Shared Care
a model for clinical management

Peter Edwards
General Practitioner, Ely Bridge Surgery, Cardiff

Stephen Jones
Service Development Manager,
Cardiff Fundholding Group

Dennis Shale
David Davies Professor of Respiratory and Communicable
Diseases, Llandough Hospital and Community NHS Trust

Mark Thursz
Lecturer in Medicine, St Mary's Hospital NHS Trust, London

Radcliffe Medical Press
Oxford and New York

Radcliffe Medical Press Ltd
18 Marcham Road, Abingdon, Oxon OX14 1AA, UK

Radcliffe Medical Press, Inc.
141 Fifth Avenue, New York, NY 10010, USA

British Library Cataloguing in Publication Data

A catalogue record for this book is available from the British Library.

ISBN 1 85775 165 5

Library of Congress Cataloging-in-Publication Data

Shared care : a model for clinical management / Peter Edwards ... [et al.]
     p.   cm.
  Includes bibliographical references (p.).
  ISBN 1–85775–165–5
   1. Health care teams—Great Britain.   2. Medical consultation—Great Britain.
3. Medical referral—Great Britain.   4. Continuum of care—Great Britain.
I. Edwards, Peter, general practitioner.
R729.5.H4S53   1996
362.1′0941—dc20   95–47038   CIP

Typeset by Advance Typesetting Ltd, Oxfordshire
Printed and bound in Great Britain

Contents

Acknowledgement

Our special thanks go to our families and professional colleagues for their support and encouragement during the writing of this book. We are particularly indebted to Dr Terry Davies and Dr Keith Freeman for their respective contributions to the sections on the DIALECTS project and teledermatology.

Introduction

The purpose of this book

Since the National Health Service began, it has developed by a combined process of evolution and revolution. From its very beginning, the tripartite NHS included primary and secondary sectors, which operated largely independent of one another and it is only in recent years that the concept of shared care has come to the fore. This book examines current developments in shared care, describes and promotes a model for shared care and offers a vision for how shared care may be developed in the future. In doing so, it attempts to explore the issues from both clinical and non-clinical perspectives. It also uses the latest modelling techniques to provide a robust framework for effective description of the components of, and the operation of, an effective shared care scheme.

Many independent observers have commented on the growth of 'jargon' within the NHS, and the authors are conscious that this book introduces and develops a number of concepts and modelling techniques that will be new to many readers, be they clinician or non-clinician. The authors have sought to overcome this by starting at a point with which most readers will be familiar and then introducing the formal modelling techniques that underpin this work. This is then developed into a flow process model, akin to an algorithm, which will be familiar to many readers. This is then 're-written' into more formal modelling language both to describe its detailed structure and to demonstrate its intellectual robustness. The authors then describe the components of care that patients receive in either of the primary or secondary care sectors, followed by an examination of how patients are transferred between these two sectors, making appropriate reference to the flow process model throughout. There is then a description of a vision for the future that considers how shared care schemes based on this model can be, and have been, implemented. Finally, we consider the importance of outcome measures.

The book emulates the health care professional's desire to meet patient needs, and to this extent ends where it begins, with a tale of a patient's interaction with the NHS (fictitious or apocryphal depending on your point of view), which the authors have described as a patient's 'health career'.

The majority of health care professionals work within teams within an establishment, such as a hospital or general practice. An effective move towards the introduction of shared care programmes will inevitably lead to extended teams working across the primary/secondary care interface. This book will help to clarify how such extended teams should function to enhance patient care within an effective shared care programme. The book, however, has deliberately eschewed the topic of drug treatments within the organization of shared care schemes. Such a topic is at once very large while also only being amenable to local solutions dependent upon circumstance and personalities.

Meeting patient needs

One of the consequences of the introduction of the internal market into the NHS has been the recognition of the patient as both the consumer and ultimate funder of the service. Health economists are keen to match the 'health needs' of the population to the available resources, with a demonstrable output.

Clinicians are taught within medical school of the history of the NHS since 1948, and are aware of the historical barriers between primary and secondary care. Patients may not recognize or approve of such divides.

Clinicians understand the background to squabbles about the provision of medication to patients who attend outpatient departments: clinicians will care about their own budgets, patients will not. Patients believe that all clinicians are working for the same NHS, which in its totality should provide the medication.

Such examples present, we believe, a powerful case for the adoption of shared care schemes that are carefully devised and implemented so that patients truly can receive 'seamless care'. The following 'case history' describes the interactions between a patient and clinicians (all of whom are fictitious) within the existing system and has been described as a 'health career'.

A patient's 'health career'

Mr Smith is a 78-year-old retired man. He presents to his general practitioner, Dr Jones, complaining of exertional dyspnoea. After obtaining a history and conducting a physical examination, Dr Jones decides to refer Mr Smith to one of the general physicians at his local district general hospital. His referral letter follows:

Dr B Jones MBBS MRCGP   The Mill Surgery
Dr A Taylor MBBS DRCOG DCH   14 Waters Lane
                                                Somertown

Dear Dr Rest

re: Mr J Smith, 44 High St, Somertown

I would be grateful if you would see this 78-year-old patient of mine, who is complaining of exertional dyspnoea. He is overweight and a heavy smoker but has had no previous cardiovascular or respiratory problems. I found no significant abnormality on examination apart from blood pressure of 160/95.

I would appreciate your opinion as to whether this is primarily a respiratory or a cardiovascular problem. I think that Mr Smith primarily has cardiac failure. If this turns out to be the case should I start him on an angiotensin-converting enzyme inhibitor?

Yours sincerely

Dr Rest sees Mr Smith and conducts a series of investigations. He writes back to Dr Jones:

Dr W Rest MBBS MRCP
Consultant Physician
Royal Victoria Hospital
Somertown

Dear Dr Jones

re: Mr J Smith, 44 High St, Somertown

Thank you for referring Mr Smith to my clinic. I felt on balance that this man's history suggested congestive cardiac failure. This was confirmed by finding mild pulmonary oedema on the chest radiograph and poor left ventricular function on echocardiography. I have started Mr Smith on co-amilofruse 5/40 one tablet once daily. I will see him again in one month.

Yours sincerely

One month later Mr Smith is reviewed in the outpatient clinic by Dr Rest's senior house officer, Dr Work. Dr Work thinks that Mr Smith should be started on an angiotensin-converting enzyme (ACE) inhibitor and therefore prescribes enalapril 5 mg once daily. Mr Smith asks Dr Work, 'Just while I'm here Doc', to look at a rash that he has developed on his arms. Dr Work, being unable to identify the rash, refers Mr Smith to Dr Hilton-Smythe, the consultant dermatologist. Dr Work checks Mr Smith's electrolytes and arranges to see him again in one month.

One month later Mr Smith is reviewed in clinic by Dr Holiday, who is Dr Work's replacement. Unfortunately, the patient's notes are missing and Mr Smith has forgotten to bring his medications with him. Dr Holiday muddles through and pieces together the clinical situation as best he can. He guesses correctly that Mr Smith has left ventricular failure and that he has been taking diuretics. Unaware that the electrolytes have recently been checked (by Dr Work and, incidentally, by Mr Smith's GP), Dr Holiday decides to check Mr Smith's electrolytes again and see him in one week to be on the safe side.

A week later Dr Holiday finds that Mr Smith's potassium is slightly raised and changes the co-amilofruse to frusemide 40 mg once daily. He arranges to see Mr Smith again in one month. Thereafter Mr Smith is seen at one to three month intervals by a series of Dr Rest's rotating senior house officers.

Some time later Dr Jones receives a letter from Dr Hilton-Smythe:

Dr E Hilton-Smythe MD FRCP
Consultant Dermatologist
Royal Victoria Hospital
Somertown

Dear Dr Jones

re: Mr J Smith, 44 High St, Somertown

Your patient was referred to me by Dr Rest's senior house officer for an opinion on a recently developed rash. His has simple eczema on his forearms and I have recommended that he use hydrocortisone 2.5% cream.

Yours sincerely

Around this time, Dr Jones has another patient, Miss Hodgkin, who is suffering from night sweats. He rings up the hospital to arrange an early appointment but finds that Dr Rest has a six-month waiting list.

Mr Smith appears to have benefited from a good standard of health care, but the use of clinical resources in this example of referral-based practice is poor. Although the general practitioner posed specific questions in his referral letter, these were only partially answered in the consultant's response. Although the general practitioner made it clear that he was willing to continue to care for the patient, Mr Smith, like many patients, became trapped in a pattern of recurring outpatient visits. Nothing was achieved at these subsequent outpatient visits that could not have been achieved by the general practitioner and his team in primary care. The plan of management for this patient is not clear at any stage to the patient or to any of his professional carers. In the absence of the hospital record, all remaining clues to the management plan evaporate completely.

In this example, the general practitioner may rightly be annoyed at being displaced as the patient's primary carer. Referral to another consultant without the consent or knowledge of the general practitioner occurs commonly in hospital outpatient practice and, as in this example, the condition may be well within the scope of a general practitioner if not the medical senior house officer. The clogging up of outpatient appointments with clinical problems that are well within the scope of general practice to manage becomes increasingly irksome when patients with new and potentially serious clinical problems have to wait for appointments.

Efficient use of clinical resources may be maximized by sharing the care of chronically ill patients between primary and secondary clinicians. In order to achieve this, it is necessary to define the interface carefully and to set criteria for moving patients from primary to secondary care and, just as importantly, from secondary to primary care. Sharing the care of patients demands a high level of communication between clinicians and requires that the clinical management plan is explicit and available to all the clinicians involved. New technology for distributing the electronic health record will ensure that this model of care can be supported.

The above, not untypical, health career permits a critical question to be asked, namely: does shared care exist now?

Does shared care exist now?

Shared care between primary and secondary sectors is a principle of management that many doctors would subscribe to, although it is difficult to achieve, as shown in the example above. In much of Europe, including the United Kingdom, there is a feeling of an imbalance between the resources separately allocated to primary and secondary care. There is a political will for movement towards increasing primary care in terms of magnitude of activity, the clinical process and extra resources at the expense of secondary care. The NHS Management Executive in 1991 anticipated that there would be considerable benefits for the NHS, the process of activity within both primary and secondary care areas and in outcomes for patients if the two care sectors were integrated. An important benefit would be the potential for reducing variations in medical practice brought about by different views as to acceptable standards of primary and secondary care, different grades of medical staff, particularly in the secondary care sector, and the different perceptions of purchasers of care. In the current system patients are twice as likely to be kept within the secondary care sector, with repeated visits to clinics, if they are seen by a junior hospital doctor rather than by a consultant.

Variation in the definition of shared care and to what extent care should be shared between primary and secondary sectors leads to a range of schemes and considerable variation in the design and operation of such schemes. A survey of the management of chronic diseases in Scotland and the North West Thames areas showed that at least half of the schemes were for the care of patients with diabetes. Such schemes were small and often initiated by consultants rather than developed jointly by health professionals in the primary and secondary health care sectors.

Large schemes have been reported for the care of patients with thyroid diseases, hypertension, rheumatoid arthritis and diabetes. Recently a care scheme for asthma, either shared or integrated between general practitioners and hospital consultants, was reported and, although no clinical differences with conventional care practice were demonstrated, there was clear patient preference for the integrated or shared care scheme.

Clearly, shared care schemes need to demonstrate improved outcomes in terms of patient care, quality of life for the patients and professional satisfaction. In addition, cost–benefit analysis is required to ensure that the gains in terms of outcomes are obtained at a reasonable or optimal cost.

Shared care schemes or clinics should not be confused with outreach clinics, which are essentially clinics located in general practice but run by consultants. There are over 700 such clinics in England and Wales yet, so far, little evidence of clinical benefit. However, because the waiting times for such clinics are shorter than in hospitals, managers are keen to promote this resource. Currently, there is little information on either the clinical effectiveness or the cost-effectiveness of outreach clinics and it is estimated that 95% of the clinics are run by consultants with very little involvement by general practitioners. This failure to understand that there are common or shared standards of care in the primary and secondary sectors may contribute to a wasted resource, both in the failure to encourage general practitioners to take part in the care of these patients together with hospital consultants, and in the inappropriate use of hospital consultant time in a general practice setting.

Shared care, in its ideal form, with an integrated approach by health professionals from primary and secondary care, aims to maintain high-quality standards of care across the interface between the two health care sectors. At the present time there is very little true shared care in terms of these elements of shared care. The authors intend to demonstrate that genuine shared care, as defined below, can be effected.

The authors' definition of shared care

Clinical management should aim to deliver high-quality care based on agreed standards. Shared care permits this objective to be delivered through the optimal use of health service resources to best meet the needs of patients.

This is most effectively achieved by primary care and secondary care clinicians having joint and contemporaneous responsibility for the patient. This contrasts with the normal referral relationship between primary care and secondary care clinicians when, at certain times, responsibility for the care of the patient is handed over from one clinician to the other.

1

Shared care – current aspects

In both the UK and the rest of Europe there is a move towards community care with a view to cost containment.[1] It has been estimated that in Germany 17% of hospital patients do not need care in a hospital. In Belgium, Ireland and the UK there has been extensive firm action to close hospitals or to change them to other uses. In France, 22 000 beds are to be closed; in The Netherlands 3800. The view of the NHS Management Executive in 1991[2] was that the integration of primary and secondary care, which were seen at that time to be organizationally separated in an uncomfortable way, would be beneficial.

Attendance and reattendance at outpatient clinics has been considered the norm. In one series, of 179 referrals, 34% of patients with rheumatoid arthritis and 10% of those with osteoarthritis made four or more visits to the clinic.[3] The patients were twice as likely to be discharged by a consultant as by a junior doctor. Communication between hospitals and general practice could be improved. In one study[4] fewer than half the questions in referral letters were answered by consultants. In another,[5] while letters from most specialties were criticized for omitting information, those from psychiatrists were criticized for being too long, i.e. they contained information that the general practitioner did not consider relevant. General practitioners[6] thought that it was important that letters from consultants should contain:

- an appraisal of the problem
- examination findings
- a management plan.

Existing shared care schemes

There are many different types of scheme in existence. In a 1994 survey[7] substantial variation was found to exist in the design and operation of shared care schemes for the management of chronic diseases such as diabetes. The survey covered Scotland (36 schemes) and North West Thames (29 schemes). Diabetic schemes were found to account for half of all schemes. Fifty-three schemes provided full information. Consultants were the sole initiators in 64%. Over one-third were started between 1990 and 1992. Most schemes involved fewer than 50 GPs and fewer than 500 patients. The larger schemes with more than 1000 patients were for thyroid disease (4), rheumatoid arthritis (2), diabetes (2), hypertension and drug use (1).

Two models for general practitioners' responsibilities emerged – routine monitoring or investigation and treatment. Only four schemes had explicit selection and discharge criteria. The most common pattern of care was an annual review in hospital with three or four visits in general practice. A shared care card was the most common method of communication, although computer-generated summaries were also used. The study also showed that consultants were sometimes ignorant of what occurred in general practice. The essence of shared care can be summarized in the concept that general practitioners remain centrally involved in the care of patients who have been referred to a specialist.

Outreach clinics

Bailey et al.[8] has concluded that outreach clinics run by consultants in general practice are here to stay, but more information on their effectiveness is needed. It is surmised that there are over 700 clinics in England and Wales. Waiting times at outreach clinics tend to be shorter, and managers accept that patients benefit because of ease of access. Only 5% of general practitioners attend such clinics.

Are existing shared care schemes effective?

Examining two of the Scottish schemes in more detail reveals that in the first, the west of Scotland shared scheme for hypertension,[9] the proportions of patients who had received complete review after two years were as follows:

- shared care   82%
- outpatient care   54%
- nurse practitioner   75%.

Blood pressure control was similar in each group. Another study in Glasgow[10] showed that direct access for hearing aid fitting can provide an adequate standard of care if clear criteria are observed and tympanometry is included in assessment. The scheme reduced patients' waiting time on an outpatient waiting list and improved patients' quality of life. Clear criteria were given to general practitioners as to whom to refer directly – those over 55 with no otological abnormality other than deafness.

Present methods

The GRASSIC[11] project represents the current state of activity in regard to shared care using paper records. In 1989 an integrated care scheme was implemented. Using a computer-based patient records system, chest physicians reviewed patients in this scheme on an annual basis. Interim reviews took place in general practice, typically every three months.

Patients were sent computer-generated questionnaires at the appropriate time, inviting them to make an appointment with their general practitioner, and asking for information about:

* symptoms

* days of restricted activity

* nights of disturbed sleep

* courses of oral steroids

* general practice consultations

* admissions for asthma.

Patients were asked to give the completed questionnaire (together with a peak flow diary card if appropriate) to their general practitioner at the consultation. Simultaneously, the patient's general practitioner was sent a separate computer-generated questionnaire, mentioning that the patient was due to attend shortly for an asthma review and enclosing a questionnaire about:

* consultations

* pulmonary function

* β_2-agonist bronchodilators and steroid courses prescribed

* changes to the patient's medication

* hospital admissions.

The general practitioner was asked to return all the documents to the consultant. The information from both questionnaires was then added to the patient's computerized record. Copies of the updated record were sent to the general practitioner, along with any suggestions from the consultant for changes in the management plan. Patients receiving conventional outpatient care were seen at their regular outpatient clinic, typically every three months. The trial was based upon normal clinical practice, so as to guide practical decisions rather than merely to acquire scientific information. Thus it was 'pragmatic' rather than 'explanatory'.

Overall, integrated care patients were at no clinical, psychological or social disadvantage through membership of such a scheme. They benefited financially and in their perceived level of asthma control. Three-quarters wanted to continue within the scheme and the reduction in direct specialist contact was not associated with worse asthma management. Regular contact with general practice, with distant consultant supervision, provided care as effectively as more conventional outpatient clinic attendance. The results suggested that, once patients have been introduced to the scheme, they too appreciate its advantages, though not without reservations. Any 'credibility gap' in patients' perceptions of integrated care is likely to be most acute among those who have become long-term attendees at outpatient clinics, hence effort should be made to establish patients' confidence in the abilities of general practitioners to manage effectively those patients with stable asthma. The general perception of hospital consultants as 'experts' and general practitioners as 'generalists' is neither easily nor quickly dispelled.

Shared care schemes – the DIALECTS project

Background

Traditionally, diabetes is divided into two categories: insulin-dependent (IDDM) and non-insulin-dependent diabetes (NIDDM). IDDM is a disease of younger people, whereas NIDDM develops after middle age. However, many of these patients will also require insulin. It is estimated that, at any one time, 30–40%[12] of diabetic patients are being treated with insulin. Estimates suggest that between 1% and 2%[13] of the population have diabetes. This means that there are approximately 750 000 diabetics in the UK, with around 5000 new cases being diagnosed every year. There is a slight preponderance of males.

Diabetic subjects are prone to specific microvascular complications of diabetes, such as retinopathy and kidney disease, and to acceleration of other arterial disease leading to increased risks of myocardial infarction, cerebrovascular accidents and peripheral vascular disease. They have a substantially increased standardized mortality ratio (SMR) compared with the general population and a reduced expectation of life.

It has also been calculated that diabetes consumes between 4% and 5% of all health care resources. In fact, 'the 1.2% of people in Wales with recognised diabetes consume greater than 4–5% of all health care resources.'[14]

The hypothesis must be that providing effective clinical surveillance for diabetic subjects would considerably reduce complications, improve the quality of life of patients and lessen the use of resources. There is now convincing evidence that good metabolic control of type 1 (insulin-dependent) diabetes reduces the incidence of microvascular complications.[15]

In practical terms, the aim must be to maintain a quality of life that is as near normal as possible, while also minimizing, or even preventing, acute and chronic complications. It should be acknowledged that good control is sometimes achieved at the expense of quality of life. Education is fundamentally important in the management of diabetes, with patients taking responsibility for their own health. Thus, the guidance must address other risk factors, such as smoking, hyperlipidaemia and control of high blood pressure, as well as endeavouring to eliminate the metabolic crises of hypo- and hyperglycaemia. Effective monitoring of the condition both by the patient and by health professionals is vital, with the added aim of identifying complications early. The British Diabetes Association (BDA)[16] puts forward the main objectives of a diabetes care programme as follows:

1   provision of appropriate education to enable all people with diabetes to acquire the necessary knowledge and skill to take responsibility for managing their own health care and to modify their lifestyle in such a way as to maximize their well-being

2   the maintenance of blood glucose control at levels that are as near physiological as possible, while at the same time aiming to achieve as normal a lifestyle as possible, through regular monitoring and appropriate management of metabolic control, thereby minimizing the likelihood of developing short-term and long-term complications

3   the identification and appropriate management of individuals with cardiovascular risk factors including:

   • smoking

   • hyperlipidaemia

   • hypertension

4   the early identification and appropriate management of individuals with long-term complications of diabetes, in order to reduce:

   • angina and myocardial infarction

   • foot ulceration and limb amputation due to peripheral vascular disease and diabetic neuropathy

- blindness and visual impairment resulting from diabetic retinopathy

- stroke and other cerebral vascular disease

- end-stage renal failure due to diabetic nephropathy

5 the strict maintenance of blood glucose control before conception and throughout pregnancy in diabetic women so as to reduce fetal loss during pregnancy, stillbirths, malformations and neonatal problems.

It is vital that patients understand their diabetes, if they are to effectively participate in its management. While the GP has overall responsibility for ensuring that all patients are involved in a planned programme of diabetes care tailored to each individual's need, the care will be a collaborative effort between a number of health professionals. The BDA recommends the setting up and maintenance of a practice register of patients with diabetes, which would ideally be computerized and possibly linked to a district diabetes register. The appropriate setting for the various elements of this care will vary according to the needs of the particular patient. Communication between the different disciplines is the key to successful care. A patient-held record can help facilitate this process.

A planned programme of diabetes care includes:

1 the assessment and initial management of newly diagnosed and rediscovered patients

2 initial stabilization and education of these patients

3 regular review and maintenance of metabolic control

4 regular review and management of cardiovascular risks factors

5 ongoing education

6 management of acute complications

7 detection and management of long-term complications. Special attention should be given to children and adolescents and all women who are considering pregnancy or are already pregnant, as well as patients with significant complications or other unusual features.

In 1989, representatives of health departments from all over Europe met with diabetologists in the Italian town of St Vincent. From this meeting evolved the St Vincent Declaration. An implementation plan published in 1993 laid down standards for diabetic care and research through-out Europe. One direct consequence of adhering to these criteria would be to compare a variety of approaches to diabetic care and subsequent outcome. The five-year clinical targets set out by the St Vincent group were:

1   to cut coronary heart disease morbidity and mortality in the diabetic population by vigorous intervention
2   to reduce new blindness due to diabetes by one-third or more
3   to reduce the number of people entering end-stage diabetic renal failure by at least one-third
4   to reduce by one-half the rate of limb amputations for diabetic gangrene
5   to achieve pregnancy outcome in diabetic women equal to that in non-diabetic women.

In the UK, the reduction of diabetic gangrene by one-half, end-stage renal failure by one-third and new blindness by one-third have been accepted as health gain targets by the year 2002.

Thus, the nature of the illness and its associated sequelae means that it is important to monitor the condition with the intention of anticipating serious consequences at best, or identifying potential hazards with constructive early intervention at worst. Evidence is available[17] to suggest that good diabetic control prevents or restricts the development of important microvascular complications. Indeed, earlier diagnosis, particularly of eye and kidney changes, can lead to prevention of blindness and renal failure.

In order to meet the needs of all patients with diagnosed diabetes there should be interactive primary and hospital-based care. Ideally, local diabetes policies that set out referral criteria for patients with diabetes and the timing and route of such referrals should be agreed. Following discussion, it may be decided that some patients should 'be the subject of shared care between the primary care and hospital diabetes team'. Ever since Hayes and Harries[18] investigated the discharge of diabetic patients into the community, the need for a diabetic patient recall system has been recognized. Also, in the current climate, there is a shift away from hospital-based care towards care in the community. Problems associated with an ageing population and a reduction in public travel facilities, as well as the development of multidisciplinary teams, have encouraged a shift of diabetic care away from the hospital environment. On the other hand, improving technologies and expertise means that not only is early identification of complications possible, but also many of these can be managed with a view to avoiding or at least postponing sinister sequelae. Retinopathy, foot problems and renal failure are good examples. In such situations, there is a need for expert input from hospital specialists. It is imperative that there is good communication both between the health professionals across specialties and at the hospital–community interface. The diabetic health visitor or community diabetic nurse has a vital role to play here. Both the chiropodist and optician need also to be able to contribute to the team.

In order to monitor the illness in individuals, there is a need for good organization of data and an efficient recall system. There is also a need for the capability to measure defined outcomes and good biochemical controls and the capacity to identify the sequelae and effectiveness of early intervention. The ideal management of the diabetic patient involves a variety of health professionals both in primary health care and in hospital.

Despite several attempts to streamline shared care in West Wales, current systems, involving paper records, do not work well. It is common for a patient to be recalled to hospital and practice clinics on consecutive weeks and then not to be seen for several months. It is often weeks before a clinical record of a patient seen in hospital, sometimes with important information, arrives at the GP's desk. These are two major deficiencies that should be resolved by having a shared electronic record.

By and large, diabetic care has been fragmented and unstructured. The development of clinical guidelines would help streamline diabetic management. The application of information technology should make for a more efficient and workable system.

Implementing the project

The above outlines the background against which the DIALECTS project was set up in East Dyfed. Both Dyfed Family Health Services Authority (FHSA) and East Dyfed Health Authority agreed to support the setting up of a shared care scheme for diabetics in the area. The purpose was to provide a coordinated carer service, which included GPs, hospital consultants, nurses, dietitians, chiropodists and psychologists. The aim was to provide a standardized service, with the ultimate goal of identifying and managing all patients with diabetes, to enable them to live as normal a life as possible.

The two principal objectives were:

1   to identify as many patients as possible with diabetes, through case finding and the ongoing GP screening programme (including new patient check-ups)

2   to manage all patients with diabetes using a planned multidisciplinary programme of care.

This included the education of patients, relatives and care staff to:

• optimize glycaemia

• identify complications early and then implement appropriate treatment

• ensure selective management of patients with specific problems

• recognize and manage specific patient factors associated with the illness.

DIALECTS was established to answer the following question: did the use of a shared electronic diabetic record improve provision of care to a diabetic population?

The underlying premise of the project was that a shared record, in which the intervention of consultant physicians, GPs, hospital, community and practice nurses was recorded would:

- facilitate teamwork

- support shared care

- enable the creation of a common card of a patient profile

- eliminate inappropriate duplication of a procedure

- provide faster and more appropriate change in the patient's condition

- use the skills of a clinical team to provide an optimum service at minimum cost.

A subsidiary intention was to determine whether the use of agreed clinical guidelines contributed to an effective system of care through:

- standardizing data collection

- standardizing emergency procedures.

It was acknowledged that one of the principal problems – the implementation of problem-orientated medical records, to which all the members of an extended clinical team had access – was insoluble unless there were substantial administrative resources made available or the appropriate application of information technology (IT). The infrastructure subsequently developed would also facilitate research activity in diabetic care.

In the long-term it is hoped that the project will develop the basis for assessing the *quality* of diabetic care in addition to the project's immediate objectives of improving the *provision* of diabetic care.

The concept of shared care is now even more important because of the recent organizational developments in the NHS. Maximizing efficiency is attractive in the provider/purchaser environment, and it should have a direct out-come of improving patient care not only by ensuring an effective call/recall system, but also by making more appropriate use of specialist services as and when required. Thus, the hospital diabetologist, for example, could spend more time with patients identified as needing more specialist attention instead of wading through unnecessarily large outpatient lists. Concurrently, the practice would have direct and easy access to specialist services, while routinely monitoring the diabetic patients on their list. The development of such a project could be a template for use in other areas within the UK.

Regard was taken of other relevant computerized record systems being developed, such as PAS (Patient Administration System), so that, in due course, the information could be easily married into other clinical and administrative systems. Also, in the development stage, other diabetic monitoring packages, such as those being proposed for hospital audit by the BDA and the Royal College of Physicians (RCP), were considered with the view to seamless integration with other system developments in Europe. The fundamental difference, however, was the input from the practice and the community, as well as the hospital.

The view was that many IT projects in the health service had been technology-led. Now, a problem had been identified and IT was being asked to offer a solution. The support from health professionals gave the project a sense of ownership and was a contrast to the traditional top-down approach, while also meeting some of the targets of the Dyfed Strategy for Health.[19]

Evaluation

The feasibility of using an electronic link for sharing clinical information and the user-friendliness of the system were issues to be evaluated. There were also some other technological issues to be put to the test, such as the effectiveness of real times, and the practical question of the ease or otherwise of training non-technological persons to use the computer effectively for clinical care.

Currently, the administration of the diabetic appointment system is fragmented. It would be easy to monitor the effectiveness of the new system in avoiding appointment clashes and improving regular recall and response to consumer demand.

However, the main product – the improvement of diabetic care – was an outcome that would need clinical evaluation over a period of time. The RCP/BDA audit package, on which the clinical record would be based, would allow easy comparison with clinical information from other projects, and this could be enhanced to a European dimension by acknowledging the European Commission guidelines. There would also be the bonus of assessing the quality and effectiveness of community diabetic care, especially in association with patient education. There would thus be some tangible measurements as well as provider and consumer subjective assessment.

Several previous paper-based attempts to streamline shared care have been unsuccessful. There is considerable anecdotal evidence of patients being recalled to hospital and practice clinics on consecutive weeks and then not being seen for several months. Investigations were often repeated in fragmented and unstructured ways and there was little evidence of good two-way information exchange. The intention was to implement an effective call and recall system based on clinical guidelines, which would improve the appropriate use of specialist services. Therefore, diabetic patients should be offered:

1 an annual 'MOT'

2 a regular follow-up programme

3 specialist investigation, when appropriate

4 an open and quick referral to a problem clinic run by a consultant

5 special care provision for children, adolescents and pregnant women.

Aggregated standardized data would be vital in auditing appropriate management of a condition that is a major consumer of health resources and a cause of considerable disability. A joint diabetic protocol for Dyfed had already been developed. This was based largely on previous work in this field and was non-contentious. For the pilot, it was decided to set up three separate units at each of three district general hospitals in the area. Four general practices with an interest in diabetes, the technological capability and, most importantly, the enthusiasm were invited to participate. It was anticipated that each unit would not be uniform in their needs and wants. Thus, there was ample scope for augmentation within each unit.

As well as the tangible outcome measures already mentioned, it was agreed that some subjective qualitative data would be sought and the following patient questionnaire was implemented.

1 How satisfied are you with your current diabetic care?

2 Where would you prefer to have check-ups:

  (a) at GP surgery with a doctor in attendance?

  (b) at GP surgery with a diabetic nurse in attendance?

  (c) at hospital?

3 How up-to-date is the information held about you?

4 Do you feel that tests were sometimes repeated unnecessarily?

5 Do you receive regular appointment notification of check-ups?

6 Would you like to see a copy of your diabetic record?

7 Do you sometimes go for long periods without being reviewed?

8 Do you sometimes have an appointment at the hospital and local clinic close together?

9   Is there a delay of information going from the hospital clinic to your doctor?

10   How regularly are you seen by your doctor/nurse about your diabetes?

Finally, at the first visit of each patient during the project, a baseline review questionnaire would register whether activities such as visual acuity testing, fundal, circulation and feet examinations, urine and blood testing, blood pressure measurement, weight and a treatment review had been carried out and recorded in the previous 12 months.

It was intended to repeat these questions at the end of the project, with the comparison forming part of the evaluation report.

Crucially, teamwork is important. Every contributing faction has a role to play, with the expertise of each group effectively contributing its own unique perspective which could be described as a 'black box' (see p.47). The advantage of the 'black box' approach focused on the outcome of each component part of the whole, rather than the individual processes therein. It was not forgotten that the ultimate goal was to improve the provision of care of diabetic patients. Hence, while it was felt inappropriate at this stage to elicit formal patient input into the project, there were many informal contacts with diabetic patients and the local BDA. Also, because the project was anticipating that patient records would be shared across an electronic link, the participating practices were asked to approach all diabetic patients for formal permission for their involvement.

The groundwork is now complete. The software has been developed and electronic links have been installed into the practices and hospital clinics. Where requested, the community diabetic nurses have been issued with notebook computers whose software utilizes a Paradox for Windows front end, linking with an Interbase database. This was the fastest and friendliest combination. It is hoped that the user-friendliness of the system will minimize the need for training.

In the short-term, the outcome measurements are fairly basic:

- does the technology work?

- do people readily use it, i.e. is it user-friendly?

- is it patient-friendly?

- does the administration work?

- do we actually reduce repetitious testing?

- does the appointment system work?

- can individual and aggregate data be accessed more easily than previously?

Mid-term outcome measurements include non-tangible factors such as well-being and convenience, as well as tangible measures such as the levels of blood sugars, HbA_1 and fructosamines and blood pressure.

In the long-term the targets are those set out in the St Vincent Declaration as described earlier in this section.

Conclusion

The RCGP Occasional Paper 67, *Shared Care for Diabetes*,[20] commented on the difficulties of measuring the success of shared care initiatives. This was largely because different criteria had been used, but also because the concept of shared care was a complex sociological phenomenon – 'the functioning of the primary/secondary care interface'. It also highlights the need for further research and suggests some possible areas, such as long-term follow-up of diabetic patients in randomized control trials, education needs of the primary health care team, the development of a database for use at the primary/secondary interface, the investigation of confidentiality issues, problems of accessibility and transfer of data with large, centralized databases.

It is hoped that the DIALECTS project will help to develop the infrastructure which will in time help clarify some of the problems, with the ultimate goal of optimal care for diabetic patients. This project represents a major change from previous practice when such schemes developed in an *ad hoc* way from open access initiatives, which are now examined further.

Open access

Open: not exclusive or limited

Access: means of approach

In the marketplace in which the NHS now operates, 'open access' (to investigations) can be taken to mean that all fundholding GPs, as commissioners, can negotiate directly with supplier departments without having to use a consultant 'middle man'. In the past only consultants (acting in their own right or as middle men for general practitioners) were able to order specific tests or investigations from other consultants, for example contrast studies or magnetic resonance imaging (MRI).

Earlier in this chapter the concept of the 'black box' was introduced. This concept can be helpful in clarifying the current situation: the tests that purchasers wish to obtain for their patients can be thought of as 'black boxes'. Purchasers have to spend money in a responsible manner. Our definition of a purchaser is a body corporate which commissions services for clinicians who can understand (and therefore use) the outcome(s) of a 'black box'.

These days it is the purchaser, or purchaser and provider combined, who determine what the purchaser can usefully commission and utilize.

Cardiology

Can open access services make a difference to the way the care is delivered? In the field of ischaemic heart disease, a 1991 report[21] discussed guidelines and a new request form that were provided by a group of cardiologists to facilitate the provision of an open access exercise electrocardiography service.

A recent survey of general practitioners by Gandhi *et al.*[22] found that the majority of patients with angina (75%) are not referred to hospital. The authors expressed surprise at this finding because the respondents to the study were mostly in agreement that exercise testing is useful for establishing the diagnosis of angina and that coronary angioplasty and coronary bypass surgery are effective in relieving symptoms. Most general practitioners thought symptom frequency and duration were important in deciding whether or not to refer a patient for cardiological investigations. This is despite the fact that there is evidence[23] that symptoms are a poor guide to disease severity and long-term prognosis.

There is also a transatlantic difference. In the UK only 50% of general practitioners believe that an exercise test is useful in assessing the prognosis of angina. In contrast,[24] in the US 81% of family physicians believe that such testing should be performed as part of the initial management of patients with angina.

A poor performance in an exercise test is associated with an increase of subsequent coronary events.[25] General practitioners seemed uncertain about the evidence relating to angioplasty or bypass surgery, which can be summed up as:

- angioplasty relieves symptoms but is associated with a restenosis rate of 25–30% within six months

- coronary artery bypass graft both relieves symptoms and improves survival in selected patients depending on the coronary anatomy.

Gandhi *et al.*[22] feel that open access to exercise electrocardiography facilities is important and should be fully evaluated bearing in mind the following:

1   data regarding the prognostic value of exercise testing in community-based angina patients, as opposed to those who have reached the tertiary centres, are scarce

2   patients presenting in the community have a threefold risk of developing unstable angina, myocardial infarction or death within two years of first presenting

3   the standards suggested by the British Cardiac Society and Royal College of Physicians are that all newly diagnosed patients with angina who are under 70 should have access to cardiological referral, with a view to exercise testing

4   cardiology outpatient departments will be swamped if all patients with stable angina are referred

5   access to cardiological investigation could be improved by allowing open access to exercise electrocardiography. As general practitioners are not generally confident in interpreting the test, the service would have to be supervised by clinicians rather than cardiac technicians

6   an open access service can provide objective data, based on exercise electrocardiography, that would allow general practitioners to retain the traditional 'gatekeeper' role based upon objective rather than subjective evidence

7   patients who achieved a low workload on treadmill testing could be prioritized for referral to a cardiologist with a view to coronary revascularization.

Gastroenterology

In gastroenterology there have been major advances in the last 20 years,[26] in part because of the development of new diagnostic technology, including fibreoptic endoscopes. Many studies, such as that of Kerrigan *et al.*,[27] have found variations in the rate of referrals from general practitioners and hospital doctors to an open access gastroscopy clinic.

One of the major areas for debate recently has been the role of *Helicobacter pylori* in both peptic ulcer and non-ulcer dyspepsia. A recent consensus conference[28] concluded that ulcer patients with *Helicobacter pylori* infection require treatment with antimicrobial agents in addition to antisecretory drugs, whether on first presentation with the illness or on recurrence.

Purchasers must determine the use to which they are going to put the result of a test (black box). In the case of endoscopy is it:

• to exclude the presence of cancer?

• to confirm the presence or absence of ulcer?

• to determine *Helicobacter pylori* status?

• to assess whether there is any oesophageal reflux?

It is important to realize that, although current open access services may have been fought for over many years, new techniques and ideas may make the use of such services less attractive.

Helicobacter pylori status may soon be routinely assessed by blood or saliva test, although at the National Institutes of Health consensus conference[28] it was felt that the value of treatment of patients with non-ulcerative dyspepsia and *Helicobacter pylori* infection remains to be determined.

Clinical practice may also change. Campbell[29] found that eradicating *Helicobacter pylori* on the basis of ulcer-like dyspepsia symptoms alone is practical and cost-effective for general practitioners. Of the patients who received eradication therapy 77% required no acid suppression or antacids in the next 11 months. Routine eradication without testing is now the norm in his practice, with the proviso of endoscoping those over the age of 45 or who complain of weight loss.

Again we must stress the importance of continual interface dialogue in determining the best way to provide care for any given group of patients. The role of open access services will have a large part to play in such a debate.

Standard setting in primary care

'Wizards don't scare me. Everyone know there's a rule that you mustn't use magic against civilians'. The man thrust his face close to Ridcully and raised a fist. Ridcully snapped his fingers. There was an inrush of air, and a croak. 'I've always thought of it more as a guideline,' he said, mildly. 'Bursar, go and put this frog in the flower bed and when he becomes his old self ...'[30]

What then are guidelines? One definition[31] is 'systematically developed statements to assist practitioner decisions about appropriate health care for specific clinical circumstances.'

The development of practice guidelines has become so popular[32] that some people speak of standardmania, although it has not been established which method is appropriate for developing valid and reliable guidelines. It is, however, important that a thorough analysis of the relevant literature is carried out, otherwise doubts will exist as to the method used for consensus and the goals and status of the guidelines are often not clear.

However, most consensus procedures do not treat the implementation of the guidelines as an integral part of the process. While the development of guidelines for general practice may be very important or even unavoidable, there is a fear that, even if doctors are informed what to do, they often do not perform according to their knowledge and skills.

There are different approaches to drawing up guidelines, each with their own advantages and disadvantages and these can now be considered further.

Decentralized approach

A local group or practice formulates guidelines on the basis of discussion and attempts consensus. Literature or local experts may be consulted. This is an educational process for the participants: it increases their sense of commitment and ownership and the chance of acceptance is good. It is often too complex for the average general practitioner and may reinforce obsolete procedures.

Centralized approach

A group of expert general practitioners develop guidelines with a national legitimacy on the basis of scientific literature and clinical experience. This may be beneficial to all general practitioners as it is increasingly difficult to keep up with medical developments.

Whichever approach is used, providers may reject guidelines that they have not been involved in producing – at the very least they may wish to reinvent them.

Since 1989 doctors in The Netherlands have been producing guidelines in conjunction with specific programmes of continuing medical education. Kahan et al.,[33] identified three different styles of guidelines:

- scholarly – based on formal quantitative literature reviews

- didactic – based on the work of peer groups

- consensual – based on the work of peer groups.

All guidelines must be founded on an adequate mixture of scientific basis, clinical applicability and feasibility in day-to-day care. The aims of the guidelines should be clearly and explicitly defined, to ensure they are:

- an aid to practice

- a tool for assessment

- a summary of available knowledge

- a way to demarcate the tasks of the general practitioner

- a support for education

- a set of criteria to evaluate the quality of care by general practitioners

- a tool for external control.

Guidelines are not self-implementing; procedures for implementation and evaluation should be built into the development of guidelines from the start (Table 1.1).

Table 1.1   Developing guidelines

Level	Aim	Body	Involvement
National, regional	Scientific basis Broad acceptance by profession	Professional organizations Experts in general practice Representatives of other bodies	Structured procedures Delphi procedures Consensus conferences
Local	Development of local guidelines and arrangements between general practitioners and other care providers	Groups of general practitioners and hospital specialists	Peer review and group consensus methods
Practice	Development of practice goals and objectives	General practitioners, other workers in the practice and patient representatives	Quality circles, structured discussion
Individual	Setting of individual objectives for quality improvements	General practitioners and peers	Self-audit and peer review

Writing guidelines

The following factors should be taken into account when written guidelines are being prepared:

- the chairman of a guideline development panel should not be an expert on the subject in question[34]

- there should be a full analysis of literature

- validity – the guidelines should lead to the expected health or cost outcomes; are guidelines based on hard evidence, clinical expertise/ preferences?

- reliability – would another group of experts produce the same guidelines?

- clinical relevance – the guidelines must be written from the perspective of problem solving within general practice

- the guidelines should be comprehensive in nature

- the guidelines should be flexible in approach.

This will allow demonstration that the guidelines:

- achieve scientific validity through a systematic analysis of the literature and through serious evaluation of the new guidelines

- acquire reliable results through formal procedures for achieving consensus and by discussing opinions and clinical experiences

- have a broad base among involved parties, thereby creating a sense of ownership through a process of development on several levels (central, local, practice, individual) with different aims.

The cost-benefit considerations of such an approach are summarized in Table 1.2.

Do guidelines work?

De Vos Meiring and Wells[36] published an evaluation of guidelines specifically for referral. The aim was to reduce referrals to a radiology department. The guidelines were sent to 150 local general practitioners who showed substantial changes in their use of the targeted investigations. In the North of England Study of Standards and Performance in General Practice,[37] guidelines were developed and implemented. All participating groups achieved improvement in prescribing and follow-up in the direction advocated by the guidelines.

Standard setting in secondary care

Standard setting in secondary care should not be an isolated process. Indeed, integration of primary and secondary care standards is an obvious prerequisite for a fully operational shared care regimen. Hence, to be effective standards have to be agreed by a number of parties including the primary and secondary care sectors and health professionals of different disciplines. In such an agreed format, guidelines may be more readily adopted and, thereby, facilitate audit and provide an interface between purchasers and providers, possibly increasing the chance of optimal cost-effectiveness.[38]

Table 1.2 Summary of incremental costs and benefits of comprehensive guidelines for selected conditions[35]

Subject	Costs	Benefits
General practitioner trainers	Time devoted to developing guidelines Time devoted to teaching guidelines	Improvements in knowledge and job satisfaction
General practitioners	Time devoted to implementing guidelines	Improvements in knowledge and job satisfaction
Patients with selected conditions	Change in pattern and cost of care	Change in clinical and social outcomes of care
Other patients	Change in number and length of consultations	Indirect changes in appropriateness of diagnosis and management
Rest of NHS	Change in the cost of drugs, investigations and referral to hospital	Improvement in training of future general practitioners

This is not easy to achieve and is dependent on the selection and quality of standards. Standards can be adopted from a variety of sources, but, ideally they should be evidence-based and be capable of audit. Therefore, an obvious source is published peer-reviewed research in a given area. An alternative source is the use of adopted consensus or guideline statements issued by authoritative bodies. Perhaps, the best-known examples in this area are the international and the British guidelines on the care of asthma. The revised version of the British guidelines, published in 1993, involved 39 participants in the drawing up of the document and they represented the following bodies: The British Thoracic Society, The British Paediatric Association, The Research Unit of the Royal College of Physicians of London, The King's Fund Centre, The National Asthma Campaign, The Royal College of General Practitioners, The General Practitioners in Asthma Group, The British Association of Accident and Emergency Medicine and the British Paediatric Respiratory Group.[39] These guidelines were presented to respiratory physicians for comment before publication. This type of document is becoming almost a standard approach now for professional groups to produce outlines of ideal management and, therefore, standards of care. However, guidelines produced on a national and therefore 'top-down' approach are not always acceptable within the profession, and there have been problems in their adoption.[40,41]

Standards of care, whatever their source, aim to address three issues:

1   the goal of ideal treatment

2   optimum care in response to genuine or perceived underfunding

3   variations in medical practice.

The major limits of the development of ideal care are likely to be ignorance, poor management, incompetence and disagreement with or disregard to established best practice. To overcome these problems health care research has been taken up by governments in many countries. In addition, medical and clinical audit has been encouraged with the extension of this to clinical effectiveness in the UK. The latter extols the use of evidence-based clinical practice on which to base management, in which a major component is precise audit of outcome. Hence, the adoption of appropriate guidelines and standards of care that are agreed and can be implemented is fundamental in the context of developing clinical effectiveness, although this may be a naïve approach.[42,43]

As implied already, guidelines may be unpopular for a variety of reasons. Their development and implementation can lead to considerable sensitivity on the part of the medical profession. A useful definition is 'clinical guidelines are systematically developed statements which assist in decision making about appropriate health care for specific clinical conditions. It is recommended that the term "clinical guideline" should apply to the general statement of principle and that the word "protocol" should cover the more detailed development of these broad principles for local application'.[44] However difficult the issues of development are, those of implementation are even greater.[41] The professional barriers range from 'lack of time', through 'lack of ownership', to 'loss of clinical freedom'. Other fundamental criticisms include:

• guidelines are intellectually suspect and reflect expert opinion, which may formalize unsound practice

• by reducing medical practice variation they may standardize to an average rather than to the best

• they inhibit innovation and prevent individual cases from being dealt with discretely

• medical legal issues are important as they may be taken to indicate standards expected of a competent colleague.

A solution to these difficulties is to allow ownership of the development and implementation by those using guidelines. Hence, the process of development may be seen as follows: scientifically-based or practice-validated guidelines can be developed at international, national or regional levels. These will contain standards of care that can then be adapted for local use in guidelines devised by those individuals who will be using them on a day-to-day basis. In this way the writing of guidelines has the individual's approach to the management of the disorder at the forefront, but includes national agreed standards of management.[45] By incorporating agreed standards and selecting appropriate end points, this approach can provide for an outcome-based audit. There is evidence that such 'ownership' of guidelines is important in implementation and that it is likely to lead to improved clinical outcomes.[45-55]

In the context of shared care, several parties need to be involved in the development of acceptable standards and guidelines. Patients or a patients' representative may be involved, as well as primary and secondary care medical and nursing staff and health visitors. Additional groups might involve school health services, pharmacists, physiotherapists and others depending on the disorder.

The agreed approach to the common management of patients in either primary or secondary care (shared care) would ensure common standards of management and could include agreed criteria for the transfer of responsibility for care. In addition, it could be constructed to allow an outcome-based interface audit for large numbers of patients to ensure that clinically effective treatments are applied and that their effectiveness is appropriate to the populations to which they are being applied. An example of how shared care could be developed can be taken from the literature relating to common chronic conditions.

In the asthma literature there is concern about the standard of both primary and secondary care. The 1991 National Asthma Attack Audit reviewed 218 general practices by a correspondence survey. The aim was to determine the frequency and characteristics of asthma attacks and to compare the management with the recommended guidelines.[56] Based on a population of 1775 patients experiencing 1805 asthma attacks during a three-month period, giving an estimated frequency of 14.3 episodes per thousand patients per year in the community, the majority (1546, 86%) of patients were managed entirely within primary care. The remainder (225, 12%) were admitted to hospital, and 34 (2%) were seen at accident and emergency departments and discharged. Two deaths were recorded. Generally the recording of clinical data was variable (Table 1.3).

Table 1.3 Clinical data on 1805 asthma attacks in primary care

	Proportion recorded (%)	
Pulse rate	968	(54)
Blood pressure	266	(15)
Respiratory rate	1143	(63)
Presence or absence of cyanosis	1275	(71)
Peak expiratory flow rate	1473	(82)
State of respiratory distress	1749	(97)

From Neville et al.[56]

Clearly, the recording of specific clinical signs could be considered as inadequate. However, use of a simple grading of severity based on the patient's level of distress was completed in 97% of cases (Table 1.4). This is in keeping with other surveys that suggest that simple standardized systems of recording information may lead to better audit information. The concern of this particular study was the failure of primary care doctors to manage asthma in accordance with nationally developed guidelines published a year before the survey. The key failing of underuse of nebulization and systemic corticosteroids is in keeping with data identified up to a decade before in the context of asthma deaths. However, there was an association between the perception of severity in clinical presentation and the proportion of patients treated with nebulized bronchodilators and systemic corticosteroids. Hence, the guidelines produced for the treatment of acute severe asthma based on hospital experience may have been an inappropriate measure by which to judge the quality of primary care. However,

Table 1.4 Severity of symptoms and management of asthma attacks

	Severity						
	Not breathless (n=248)	Mildly breathless (n=900)	Breathless and distressed (n=535)	Too breathless to talk (n=68)	Moribund (n=2)	Not recorded (n=56)	Total (n=1805)
Managed exclusively by general practitioner	243	840	401	33	2	27	1546
Given nebulized bronchodilator	28	197	217	27	1	7	477
Given systemic steroids	54	556	208	28	0	17	863
Managed in and discharged from accident and emergency department*	3	10	14	2	0	5	34
Given nebulized bronchodilators	1	5	10	1	0	4	21
Given systemic steroids	1	3	6	1	0	3	14
Admitted to hospital†	2	50	120	33	0	24	225
Given nebulized bronchodilators	2	23	66	22	0	13	126
Given systemic steroids	1	20	59	24	0	12	116

* Incomplete information supplied for eight patients.
† Incomplete information supplied for 70 patients.

a considerable proportion of patients considered to be breathless and dis-
tressed and too breathless to talk did not receive recommended life-saving
therapy (Table 1.4). There were also differences in the maintenance treatment used before and after attacks and also a failure to follow-up changed
treatment after an acute episode (Table 1.5). The reasons why the guidelines
were not being adopted and were not in use are not clear. It may be that
they appeared to be unrealistic for practical implementation in general
practice; however, it did indicate that the implementation of guidelines
requires that they are simple, practical and capable of implementation.[57]
Their development and dissemination needs to be supported by educational
initiatives and help with implementation within the context of individual
practices and their population.[58]

Table 1.5 British Thoracic Society (BTS) steps before and after attacks in patients managed
solely by general practitioners (n=1546*)

Step	No. (%) patients receiving maintenance treatment		No. (%) with change in maintenance treatment after attack	
	Before attack	After attack	Unchanged or step down	Step up
0	349 (23)	53 (3)	55 (15)	298 (85)[†]
1	374 (24)	282 (18)	147 (39)	227 (61)
2	356 (23)	494 (32)	275 (77)	81 (23)
3	303 (20)	504 (33)	281 (93)	23 (7)
4	107 (7)	155 (10)	104 (97)	3 (3)
5	51 (3)	52 (3)	51	

Children were placed on equivalent 'BTS step' according to prescribed prophylactic medication.
* Medication details incomplete in six patients.
† A total of 131 (38%) patients stepped up from step 0 to step 1 (bronchodilators as required) and
161 (46%) from step 0 to step 2 or beyond (prophylactic medication).

There are several studies showing major differences in the management
of patients with asthma between those under the care of specialist chest
physicians and those without specialist respiratory input.[59–62] There still
remain questions regarding the quality of care in hospital ranging from first
attendance at the accident and emergency department, through inpatient
care to discharge. Protocols have been developed to attempt to improve the
care of patients admitted to hospital. Lim and Harrison[63] reported on their
experience during a 13-month period during which they aimed to compare
practice against recommendations (Table 1.6). They audited 78 acute admissions with asthma all coming under the care of one consultant respiratory physician. They were able to demonstrate that a complete objective

Table 1.6   Results of a nine-item audit of asthma care performed for 78 admissions in two audit periods

Audit measures	Period 1 1/1/90 to 31/8/90 (n=55)	Period 2 1/12/90 to 31/1/91 (n=23)
Preadmissions		
1 Reason for deterioration of asthma	51 (93%)	23 (100%)
2 Peak expiratory flow (PEF) preadmission	42 (76%)	17 (74%)
3 Systemic steroids	39 (71%)	19 (83%)
Inpatient		
4 Full objective assessment of severity	54 (98%)	23 (100%)
5 PEF variability in the 24 hours before discharge	[<20%] 30 (55%)	[<20%] 17 (74%)
Predischarge		
6 Written check on inhaler technique	32 (58%)	22 (96%)
7 Oral steroids on discharge	54 (98%)	22 (96%)
8 PEF meter for home monitoring	43 (78%)	19 (83%)
9 Outpatient appointment within four weeks	33 (60%)	13 (57%)

Reproduced with permission from Lim K L and Harrison B D W (1992) A criterion based audit of npatient asthma care. *J. Royal College Physicians of London.* **26**: 71–5.

assessment of the severity of the patient was performed in 77 of the 78 patients. The failure in one patient was because of the patient's age. In the first period of the audit the percentage of patients who had achieved a variability of less than 20% in their peak expiratory flow rate in the 24 hours preceding discharge had risen from 55% to 74%. Other indicators also increased. This audit had some value in that patients were perceived to have been better cared for, criteria for discharge were modified and more carefully documented assessment of inhaler technique was carried out.

Hence, there is considerable room for improvement in the standard of care for asthma in both the primary and secondary care sectors. The favoured approach is to evolve the quality of care upwards by developing shared care protocols which recognize, by agreement with all parties, that care has to be given to an agreed standard. Crucial to this agreement is the concept that if local standards can be set by local adaptation of nationally produced guidelines, this process may lead to a better uptake of guidelines. Attempts have been made to produce integrated or shared care schemes for patients with asthma both in The Netherlands and in the UK. The success of such schemes depends upon the agreement of general practitioners and hospital consultants to cooperate in not only the development of a process, but its implementation and full audit. The experience of both the Dutch and

UK groups suggests that integrated care is acceptable to primary care practitioners, the patients and hospital consultants.[64,65]

Structure, process and outcome

Clinical medicine has entered a phase in its evolution in which audit (defined as a careful, detailed and often formal study designed to uncover pertinent information) is increasingly being adopted. Many types of audit have been described – medical, nursing, managerial, clinical etc. – but it is becoming clear that there will be an increasing need for multidisciplinary audit, to include nurses, paramedics and managers;[66] and indeed, in some parts of the USA, the use of multidisciplinary groups to decide on appropriateness is becoming the standard.[67]

The authors contend that shared care is a multidisciplinary activity. It is important for all groups to be involved in audit because a study in the north of England demonstrated that only those doctors actively involved in standard setting subsequently changed their clinical behaviour.[68]

The next question is what should be audited, regardless of clinical topic. As long ago as 1966, Donabedian[69] proposed three criteria by which the quality of medical care might be evaluated:

1   structure – the resources available to the doctor

2   process – what the doctor does to or for the patient

3   outcome – the resulting changes in the health of the patient.

This may be thought of as a hierarchical list demonstrating increasing complexity.

Structure

This is most useful when taking a minimalist approach. It is possible to predict what cannot be done if certain accommodation or equipment is not available. The converse is not true. The fact that a clinician has access to a piece of equipment does not guarantee that it will be used correctly or at all.

Process

Counting has its uses, especially when comparing activity at multiple sites. However, the fact that a patient has undergone a process does not guarantee that the process has been technically successful or that the patient will benefit from it.

Outcome

As Ellwood[70] has pointed out, measurement of outcomes is likely to become an increasingly important part of medical care evaluation. Few activities that are currently undertaken are measured by outcome. One often quoted example is that of childhood immunization. Target rates are set, however, not for the number of children who seroconvert, but for the number of children who are immunized. In this example it is assumed that process is equivalent to outcome. The medical outcomes study[71] has suggested the following as possible outcome measurements:

- clinical end points

- physical and social functioning

- patient's health status.

Clinicians have a long tradition of defending their 'clinical freedom'; but this cannot be seen as a licence to do purely as they wish. Clinical autonomy within a managed organization requires the acceptance of mutually agreed outcome measures between clinicians and managers, together with demonstration of their achievement.

Outcome measures for asthma in a shared care setting have two main origins: patient and health professional derived. Shared care, particularly based on an electronically distributed case note system (discussed further in Chapter 7) enhances the opportunity for patient involvement.

The synthesis of a mutually exclusive state of satisfactory or unsatisfactory, in which the latter takes precedence whether by patient or health professional assessment, means that patients are equal partners in standard setting for themselves as individuals. Outcomes are therefore based upon a personalized definition of a required health status. This offers patients a greater share-holding in their management than is usually accepted by the health professions. This change, which is implicit in systems such as SCAMP, (the Shared Care Asthma Management Project described in Chapter 7), will affect the simple clinical algorithm based on medical/nursing perceptions of management of asthma and will probably change the pattern of practice.

Health professionals base their concepts of outcome on the improvement of symptoms and objective indicators of improvement. The current version of the UK asthma guidelines, and the international set, emphasize outcomes in terms of clinical parameters readily understood by various health professional groups.[38] For the management of chronic respiratory disease in adults, both asthma and chronic obstructive pulmonary disease (COPD), a series of pragmatic outcomes has been recommended (Tables 1.7 and 1.8). These outcomes consist of an ideal attainment of complete reversal of asthma symptoms with a reduction in exacerbations and no

Table 1.7   Outcome of steps 1–3: control of asthma

- minimal (ideally no) chronic symptoms, including nocturnal symptoms
- minimal (infrequent) exacerbations
- minimal need for relieving bronchodilators
- no limitations on activities including exercise
- circadian variation in peak expiratory flow (PEF) <20%
- PEF >80% of predicted or best
- minimal (or no) adverse effects from medicine

limitations on lifestyle including exercise for those with mild to moderate severity disease (steps 1–3). Objective criteria of outcome are also given, which can be incorporated into agreed self-management plans. The latter process is a focal point for patient and professional agreement on outcome measures. In essence, the patient can use a 'pick list' to reach an agreement with the health professional. For more severe asthma (Table 1.8) it is harder to be so dogmatic, and the professionals and patients may have to accept softer criteria of outcome as aims, largely based around the principle of 'least' rather than 'minimal or no symptoms'.

Table 1.8   Outcome of steps 4 and 5: best results possible

- fewest possible symptoms
- least possible need for relieving bronchodilators
- least possible limitation of activity
- least possible variation in PEF
- best PEF
- fewest adverse effects from medicine

Indicators of outcome in COPD[72]

The outcome of medical care can be assessed over short and long periods of time. Short-term measures may be useful to assess the effectiveness of management of an acute exacerbation. However, since the condition is chronic long-term measures are more useful for evaluating the overall effectiveness of medical services. Because the NHS demands immediate measurement and is not prepared to wait for long-term outcomes to be ascertained, it is necessary to adopt proxies that appear to have predictive long-term value.

Moderate COPD

These patients have some symptoms but too few to usefully measure a significant loss of lung function and significant numbers of exacerbations. Possible short-term outcome measures include:

• employment status or whether fit for normal activities

• number of exacerbations (defined as GP scripts for antibiotics per year).

Long-term outcome predictors include:

• smoking status

• change in FEV_1 over five years as a marker of progress. Accelerated loss of FEV_1, i.e. >50 ml/year, suggests almost certain severe future disability.

Severe COPD

These patients have many symptoms, grossly abnormal physiology and frequent exacerbations and hospital admissions.
   Short-term measures include:

• number of exacerbations (defined as GP scripts for antibiotics per year) or the number of admissions per year (e.g. as averaged across the general practice population)

• proportion readmitted to hospital within three months of an index (first in an episode) admission; this tests the effectiveness of hospital care, GP and social services

• an index of severity of symptoms and level of functioning

• smoking (as before)

• the absolute level of FEV_1 which measures severity as well as being a predictor of outcome.

For these patients, as with all other groups we have described, the optimal system of shared care allows the patient, the general practitioner and the consultant to jointly contribute to the care of the individual patient. In the case of chronic asthma, an example would be a patient with a peak flow greater than 80% of predicted but who has symptoms of breathlessness on exertion and rates the health status as unsatisfactory while the patient's physician deems it to be satisfactory. For the health professional there are two possible approaches in this situation. The patient may not under-stand the conceptual framework of the health professional, and a clear explanation of what can or cannot be realistically expected may be all that is needed. Alternatively, the diagnosis or elements of the diagnosis may need reassessment and therefore the option of further investigation may need to be pursued. The former option of better communication with agreed management strategies and outcomes is likely to be a major effect of a formal shared care scheme, e.g. for asthma. This will allow patients with chronic asthma who have concerns about the level and nature of their treatment to achieve an agreed level of 'normality'. This avoids the health professionals' aims for a complete return to normal lung function con-flicting with the patients' needs and desire not to feel chronically ill. This compromise between feeling 'normal' on the level of medication probably explains the stoicism found in patients with asthma and the delays often reported in seeking help.[73]

References

1 Abel-Smith B, Mossialos E (1994) Cost containment and health care reform. A study of the European Union. *Occasional Paper in Health Policy No. 2*. LSE Health, London School of Economics and Political Science, London.

2 NHS Management Executive (1991) *Integrating Primary and Secondary Health Care*, EL (91) 27. Department of Health, London.

3 Sullivan F, Hoare T (1990) New referrals to rheumatology clinics – why do they keep coming back? *Br J Rheumatol* **29**, 53–57.

4 Jacobs L G H, Pringle M A (1990) Referral letters and replies from orthopaedic departments: opportunities missed. *Br Med J* **301**, 470–473.

5 Craddock N, Craddock M (1989) Psychiatric discharge summaries: differing requirements of psychiatrists and general practitioners. *Br Med J* **299**, 1382.

6 Newton J, Eccles M, Hutchinson A (1992) Communication between general prac-titioners and consultants: what should their letters contain? *Br Med J* **304**, 821–824.

7 Hickman M, Drummond N, Grimshaw A (1994) The operation of shared care for chronic disease. *Hlth Bull* **52**, 118–126.

8 Bailey J, Black M, Wilkin D (1994) The special branch. *Hlth Serv J* **104**(5413), 30–31.

9 McGhee S M, McInnes G T, Hedley A J et al. (1994) Co-ordinating and standardizing long term care: evaluation of the west of Scotland shared scheme for hypertension. *Br J Gen Pract* **44**, 441–445.

10 Swan I R C, Browning G G (1994) A prospective evaluation of direct referral to audiology departments for hearing aids. *J Laryngol Otol* **108**, 120–124.

11 GRASSIC (1994) Integrated care for asthma; a clinical, social and economic evaluation. *Br Med J* **308**, 559–564.

12 British Diabetes Association (1991) *Minimal Education Requirements for the Care of Diabetes in the UK*. BDA, London.

13 Fleming D M (1994) Diabetic registers in general practice. *Br Med J* **308**, 134.

14 Strategic Management Division (1991) *Contracting for Health: Diabetes Mellitus*. Report for the Welsh Medical Committee by the Working Party on Diabetes. Welsh Office Health Dept, Cardiff.

15 DCCT (1993) Treatment of diabetes and the development and progression of long term complications in IDDM. *N Engl J Med* **329**, 977.

16 Royal College of Physicians Committee on Endocrinology and Diabetes Mellitus and British Diabetes Association (1984) *The Provision of Medical Care for Adult Diabetic Patients in the United Kingdom*. Royal College of Physicians, London.

17 Diabetic Control and Complications Research Group (1993) The effect of complications in insulin-dependent diabetes mellitus. *N Engl J Med* **329**, 977–986.

18 Hayes T M, Harries J (1984) Randomised control trial of routine clinical care versus routine practice care for type 2 diabetics. *Br Med J* **289**, 728–730.

19 East Dyfed Health Authority and Dyfed FHSA (1991) *Local Strategies for Health: The Next Steps*. East Dyfed Health Authority, Dyfed.

20 Greenhalgh P M (1994) *Shared Care for Diabetes*. Royal College of General Practitioners, London.

21 Sulke A N, Paul V E, Taylor C J et al. (1991) Open access exercise electro-cardiography: a service to improve the management of ischaemic heart disease by general practitioners. *J Roy Soc Med* **84**, 590–594.

22 Gandhi M, Lampe F, Wood D (1955) Management of angina pectoris in general practice: a questionnaire survey of general practitioners. *Br J Gen Pract* **45**, 11–13.

23 Hultgren H, Peduzzi P (1984) The Veterans Administration co-operative study of surgery for coronary artery occlusive disease. Relation of severity of symptoms to prognosis in stable angina pectoris. *Am J Cardiol* **54**, 988–993.

24 Hartz A, Hartz P, Bartholomew M et al. (1989) How physicians use the stress test for the management of angina. *Med Decision Making* **9**, 57–61.

25 Weiner D, Ryan T, McCabe C *et al.* (1991) Prognostic importance of a clinical profile and exercise test in medically treated patients with coronary artery disease. *J Am Coll Cardiol* **3**, 772–779.

26 Forgacs I (1995) Recent advances – clinical gastroenterology. *Br Med J* **310**, 113–116.

27 Kerrigan D D, Brown S R, Hutchinson G H (1990) Open access gastroscopy: too much to swallow? *Br Med J* **300**, 374–376.

28 National Institutes of Health consensus conference (1994) *Helicobacter pylori* in peptic ulcer disease. *JAMA* **344**, 39–40.

29 Campbell L M (1994) *Br J Med Econ* **7**, 147–153.

30 Pratchett T (1994) *Soul Music*. Victor Gollancz, London.

31 Field M J, Lohr K N (1990) *Clinical Practice Guidelines: Direction of a New Agency*. Institute of Medicine, Washington DC.

32 Grol R (1993) Development of guidelines for general practice. *Br J Gen Pract* **43**, 146–151.

33 Kahan J P, Kanouse D E, Winkler J D (1988) Stylistic variations in National Institutes of Health consensus statements, 1979–1983. *Int J Technol Assess Health Care* **4**, 289–304.

34 Smith A (1991) In search of consensus: no agreement on who should write guidelines or how they should be used. *Br Med J* **302**, 800.

35 Russell I T *et al.* (1990) Performance review in British primary health care: an epidemiological and economic evaluation. In *Primary Health Care* (ed. P Bergerhoff *et al.*). Springer, Berlin.

36 De Vos Meiring P, Wells I P (1990) The effect of radiology guidelines for general practitioners. *Radiology* **42**, 327–329.

37 North of England Study of Standards and Performance in General Practice. Medical audit in general practice. *Br Med J* **304**, 1480–1488.

38 National Health Service Executive (1993) *Improving Clinical Effectiveness*. EL (93) 115. HMSO, London.

39 Pearson M G, Partridge M R, Harrison B D W (1993) Guidelines on the management of asthma. *Thorax* **48**, S1–S24.

40 Drummond M F, Maynard A (1993) *Purchasing and Providing Cost Effective Healthcare*. Churchill Livingstone, Edinburgh.

41 Delamothe T (1993) Wanted: guidelines that doctors will follow. *Br Med J* **307**, 218.

42 Morrison I, Smith R (1994) The future of medicine. *Br Med J* **309**, 1099–1100.

43 McKee M, Clarke A (1995) Guidelines, enthusiasms, uncertainty, and the limits to purchasing. *Br Med J* **310**, 101–104.

44 Clinical Resource and Audit Group (1993) *Clinical Guidelines*. Scottish Office, Edinburgh.

45 Grimshaw J M, Russell I T (1993) Effect of clinical guidelines on medical practice: a systematic review of rigorous evaluations. *Lancet* **342**, 1317–1322.

46 Collier J, Picton C, Littlejohns P (1994) Coordinating locally 'owned' treatment guidelines. *J Roy Coll Phys Lond* **28**, 519–522.

47 Hopkins J A, Shoemaker W C, Greenfield S *et al.* (1980) Treatment of surgical emergencies with and without an algorithm. *Arch Surg* **115**, 745–750.

48 Linn B S (1980) Continuing medical education: impact on emergency room burn care. *JAMA* **244**, 565–570.

49 Barnett G O, Winickoff R N, Morgan M M *et al.* (1983) A computer-based monitoring system for follow-up of elevated blood pressure. *Med Care* **21**, 400–409.

50 McDonald C J, Hui S L, Smith D M *et al.* (1984) Reminders to physician from an introspective computer medical record: a two year randomized trial. *Ann Intern Med* **100**, 130–138.

51 Wilson D M, Taylor D W, Gilbert R *et al.* (1988) A randomized trial of a family physician intervention from smoking cessation. *JAMA* **260**, 1570–1574.

52 Cohen S J, Christen A G, Katz B P *et al.* (1987) Counselling medical and dental patients about cigarette smoking: the impact of nicotine gum and chart reminders. *Am J Public Health* **77**, 313–316.

53 Cohen S J, Stookey G K, Katz B P *et al.* (1989) Encouraging primary care physicians to help smokers quit: a randomized trial. *Ann Intern Med* **110**, 686–752.

54 Cummings S R, Coates T J, Richard R J *et al.* (1989) Training physicians in counselling about smoking cessation: a randomised trial of the "Quit for Life" program. *Ann Intern Med* **110**, 640–647.

55 North of England Study of Standards and Performance in General Practice (1992) Medical audit in general practice: effects on doctors' clinical behaviour and the health of patients with common childhood conditions. *Br Med J* **304**, 1480–1488.

56 Neville R G, Clark R C, Hoskins G *et al.* (1993) National asthma attack audit 1991–2. *Br Med J* **306**, 559–562.

57 Haines A, Feder G (1992) Guidance on guidelines. *Br Med J* **305**, 705–706.

58 Keeley D (1993) How to achieve better outcome in treatment of asthma in general practice. *Br Med J* **307**, 1261–1263.

59 Osman L M, Abdalla M I, Beattie J A G *et al.* (1994) Reducing hospital admission through computer supported education for asthma patients. *Br Med J* **308**, 568–571.

60 Bucknall C E, Robertson C, Moran F *et al.* (1988) Differences in hospital asthma management. *Lancet* **i**, 748–750.

61 Baldwin D R, Ormerod L P, Mackay A D *et al.* (1990) Changes in hospital management of acute severe asthma by thoracic and general physicians in Birmingham and Manchester during 1978 and 1985. *Thorax* **45**, 130–134.

62 Bell D, Layton A J, Gabby J (1991) Use of a guideline based questionnaire to audit hospital care of acute asthma. *Br Med J* **302**, 1440–1443.

63 Lim K L, Harrison B D W (1992) A criterion based audit of inpatient asthma care. *J Roy Coll Phys Lond* **26**, 71–75.

64 Grampian Asthma Study of Integrated Care (1994) Integrated care for asthma: a clinical, social, and economic evaluation. *Br Med J* **308**, 559–564.

65 Van Damme R, Drummon N, Beattie J *et al.* (1994) Integrated care for patients with asthma: views of general practitioners. *Br J Gen Pract* **44**, 9–13.

66 Moss F, Smith R (1991) From audit to quality and beyond. *Br Med J* **303**, 199–200.

67 Gottlieb L K, Margolis C Z, Schoenbaum C S (1990) Clinical practice guidelines at an HMO: development and implementation in a quality improvement model *Qual Rev Bull* **16**, 80–86.

68 Centre for Health Services Research Ambulatory Care Programme (1991) *North of England Study of Standards and Performance in General Practice.* Department of Health, London.

69 Donabedian A (1966) Evaluating the quality of medical care. *Millbank Memorial Fund Quarterly* **44**, 166–206.

70 Ellwood P M (1988) Outcomes management: a technology of patient experience. *N Engl J Med* **318**, 1549–1556.

71 Tarlov A R, Ware J E, Greenfield S *et al.* (1989) The medical outcomes study. An application of methods for monitoring the results of medical care. *JAMA* **282**, 925–930.

72 Pearson M (ed.) (1995) *Guidelines for the Management of Chronic Obstructive Pulmonary Disease.* Statement from the BTS. In preparation.

73 Sibbald B (1989) Patient self care in acute asthma. *Thorax* **44**, 97–101.

2

An introduction to modelling

What is a model?

Clinicians are used to working with models, although they rarely use the term explicitly. The models that clinicians are most familiar with are those of disease processes, which are built up from immunological, microbiological and pathological observations about the disease. It is the purpose of clinical research to attempt to disprove the model or an aspect of the model. When a well-executed piece of research fails to disprove the model, the model is strengthened, and when the research succeeds in disproving the model it must be replaced or revised. As an example, the model of asthma describes an inflammatory condition of the respiratory tract caused by a hyperactive immunological response to non-pathogenic antigens. This leads to the obstruction of airflow owing to bronchial smooth muscle contraction and an inflammatory infiltrate. This model allows the prediction that asthmatic symptoms will respond to anti-inflammatory medication (steroids) and drugs that reduce smooth muscle contraction (β-agonists). The fact that these drugs do indeed ameliorate asthma supports the validity of the disease model.

Although clinicians are familiar with the type of model illustrated above, they are not usually familiar with the concept of enterprise modelling. Such models are representations of the real world that are used in business as well as in other contexts to visualize complex situations. Enterprise models are used to facilitate communication between parties from diverse professional backgrounds by providing a common 'language'. A simple example of an enterprise model is a scale model used by architects when communicating about a building to potential clients or to builders. Modelling removes unnecessary fine details and shrinks the real world down to a level of complexity which is readily understood by the users. Enterprise models are used to design and test real world structures and organizations on a small scale in the same way that scale models of cars and aircrafts are used to test designs in wind tunnels.

There are a wide variety of modelling techniques in use, but some enterprise business modellers have found it useful to use a broad category of techniques created by the systems analysis profession. Originally these techniques were developed to aid in the design and specification of computer systems, but they have now found an equally important function in the representation of businesses. Enterprise models developed with systems analysis techniques are used to plan business ventures and to analyse problems with business practices, in addition to the original function of specifying computer systems to support some of the business functions.

Early systems analysis techniques were sufficiently esoteric as to require extensive training in their use. These techniques were not accessible to business users and, therefore, not appropriate for use as communication tools beyond the boundary of computer specification. Even when the analysis techniques became more accessible, there remained a heavy bias towards representation of processes (e.g. making sales, hiring employees or creating a product) rather than of structure (e.g. equipment, employees or products) that was inappropriate to business users who needed a more balanced approach. In the 1980s a new flavour of analysis techniques emerged, which were more accessible to business users and more pertinent to enterprise modelling; these are the object-oriented analysis techniques. A number of related object-oriented analysis techniques have now been developed, but they are conceptually very similar and focus on the structure of organizations and the way in which the structure changes with time rather than on process. By analogy with the human body this is akin to representing the body in terms of its component parts, e.g. heart, lungs and kidneys, as opposed to a representation that focused on circulation, ventilation and excretion. Neither method is wholly correct, but the former is more intuitive and therefore facilitates communication.

The object-oriented modelling technique

This description of the object-oriented analysis technique is a broad overview based on the technique developed by John Edwards and recently published by James Martin and Jim Odell.[1] There are many other, mainly eponymous, object-oriented analysis techniques that differ principally in the syntax used to present the model. In order to maintain reasonable brevity illustrative examples have been given in the text, and it is anticipated that the reader will derive a general understanding by reference to the accompanying figures.

Object-oriented analysis uses our natural propensity to put the objects in our environment into pigeonholes. We naturally group objects and people together in an attempt to simplify our surroundings. In medicine it might be said, for instance, that such and such a patient is a diabetic; this does not imply that the patient is identical to all other diabetics or that the disease will behave in exactly the same way as in any other diabetics. In object-oriented analysis each of these pigeonholes, which are called *concepts*, is given a label. Because analysis techniques need to be precise, each concept has a definition. Thus, all objects in the real world that satisfy the conditions of the concept definition are classified as being instances of the concept (Figure 2.1).

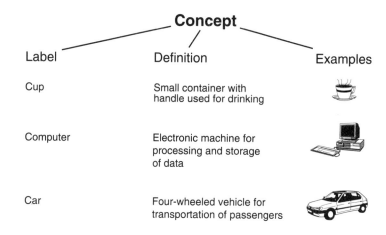

Figure 2.1   Concepts.

The structure of an organization can be represented as a *concept diagram*, with each of the identification concepts represented by a box containing the concept label. *Relationships* or associations between objects in the real world are represented by lines drawn between the concepts on a concept diagram. As an example (Figure 2.2) one might create a concept diagram

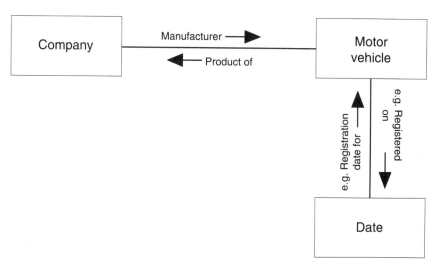

Figure 2.2   Concepts and relationships.

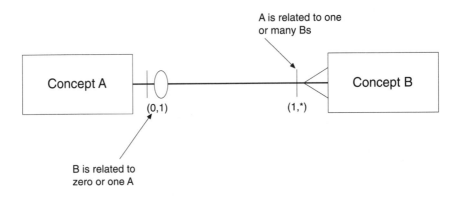

Figure 2.3   Concept diagram cardinality syntax.

with 'motor vehicle' as one concept and 'company' as a second. A line drawn between them could represent the relationship 'manufacturer'. However, lines between concepts should have meaning no matter in which direction they are read; thus, in this example, the company manufactures the car in one direction and the car is a product of the company in the opposite direction. To add precision to the model each relationship should be named to avoid confusion. It can be seen that if a relationship is drawn between motor vehicle and the concept 'date' this might represent date of manufacture, date of registration or the date for its next service.

In real life the relationships between concepts are often numerically constrained (a motor car has one and only one engine). These constraints are represented diagrammatically as cardinalities, which denote the maximum and minimum number of concept As that relate to concept Bs (Figure 2.3).

One of the tools used in analysis to simplify the domain is a process called generalization (Figure 2.4). Generalization finds common properties (relationships) shared by two or more concepts, which can then be given to a parent concept. Thus, table, chair and cupboard may have a parent concept furniture holding the common relationships of all these items which might be manufacturer and material. Through generalization, models may develop several hierarchies of concepts, and it should be remembered that low-level concepts inherit properties from all the concepts that are higher up the generalization tree.

The opposite of generalization is *subclassification*, which allows us to increase the detail in the model. Subclassification must be performed on a logical basis such that all subclasses of the parent concept are mutually exclusive (e.g. person could be subclassified to man or woman). Subclasses are held diagrammatically in a box called a partition. When all possible subclasses in the partition have been catalogued the partition is said to be complete, and when only the immediately relevant subclasses are catalogued the partition is said to be left incomplete. In some circumstances it may be necessary to subclassify a concept on more than one basis so that, for

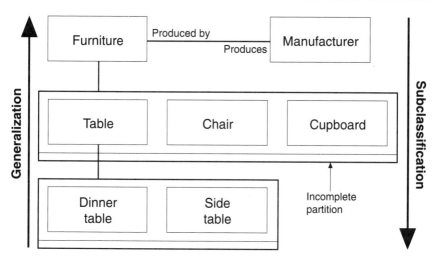

Figure 2.4   Subclassification and generalization.

instance, a person may in one subclassification be a man or woman and in a second subclassification be a doctor, a nurse or a physiotherapist.

A finished concept diagram often gives the impression of being a complete representation of the domain. However, no domain is completely static so the model must include a representation of how the concepts and relations change over time. This dynamic representation is called an *event diagram* (Figure 2.5). Processes are represented on an event diagram by boxes, which are labelled as clearly as possible with the name of the process. At the end of each process box is a small triangle representing the

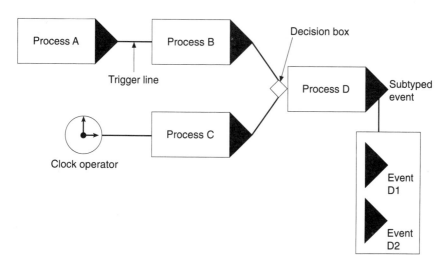

Figure 2.5   Event diagram.

completion of the process – an event. Events conclude the process to which they are attached, but the concluding event may be subtyped to represent the different ways in which a process may terminate, e.g. driving to London may terminate when London is successfully reached or when the car breaks down. When an event occurs, one of the objects represented by the concepts on the concept diagram is changed. There are only a limited number of changes that can occur:

- an object may be created
- an object may be destroyed
- a relationship between one object and another may be created
- relationships may be removed
- relationships may be transferred to other objects.

An event gives rise to a trigger line, which initiates the next process at the end of the line. When the trigger for a new process to start is a time schedule this can be represented diagrammatically by a clock symbol. Coordination and control of many processes may also be represented by the use of a diamond-shaped decision box in front of the process. The decision box should be annotated with the conditions to be satisfied before the next process may be initiated. Each event diagram deals with a limited number of events that may occur within a specified domain, and the scope will be defined explicitly by the initiating and goal events. Event diagrams should be supported by accompanying literature that details the changes occurring to objects on the concept diagram each time an event takes place.

An event diagram follows the progress of a key object over a period of time by considering that each time an important process is completed the object changes state. If, for example, we followed the progress of a patient through a casualty department (Figure 2.6) we would start with a person with symptoms. Acquiring the symptoms is outside the scope of the casualty department and would therefore be marked as an external event; nevertheless, the acquisition of symptoms is an important event that is the trigger for all subsequent events. The initial state of the patient is therefore a person with symptoms; the first state of change is, therefore, in terms of a model, the creation of a patient. A series of events would now occur in logical order: the patient would register at reception and then be sent to see the triage nurse. Now the patient is registered and triaged and therefore in an appropriate state to be assessed. When an assessment cubicle becomes free the patient is undressed and put on a trolley and a set of observations are then taken. The patient will be clerked by the casualty officer, a set of investigations will be performed and the patient given some treatment. Finally, the patient will be either discharged or referred on to a specialist team. Each

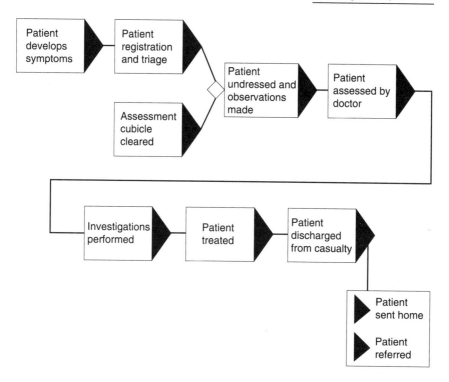

Figure 2.6   Event diagram example.

change in state, recorded by an event on the event diagram, represents an addition or removal of attributes on the concept diagram.

The advantages of using object-oriented techniques

The principal advantage of using an object-oriented analysis technique is the ability to represent a business domain in such a way that the model can be used as a vehicle for communication for parties with different professional backgrounds. An important but apparently hidden benefit of these analysis techniques is that they are fairly intuitive and therefore rapidly taught. The implication of this is that professional users (known as 'domain experts') can pick up the technique and apply it to their area of work, focusing on their own knowledge to represent the domain as a model. In a second scenario where the domain expert communicates to a professional analyst, important information may be lost and this may not be appreciated by either the analyst or the domain expert. An NHS Executive sponsored project (the Cosmos Project) to represent the clinical process succeeded by using a combination of clinicians and professional analysts working in tandem, using object-oriented techniques.

In order to understand fully the benefits of using object-oriented techniques in information systems, we must examine some technical aspects of computer system development. There are three principal phases to development:

1   the first phase is the analysis work, which produces a model of the domain that the system is to support. The model has two purposes: the first is to select which functions in the current domain could be replaced by information technology; and the second purpose is to represent the data structures and functionality of the domain that must be replicated by the computer system

2   the second phase of the analysis is to design the computer system in terms of both hardware and software

3   the final phase of development is the encoding of the design to produce the application software.

Traditional computer development techniques involved different teams working on the three different phases with inevitable loss of information at the interface between the phases. Although the enterprise model may have been used as a guide to computer system development, there is rarely a direct link between the model and its implementation. In the object-oriented paradigm the link between the model and the final implementation can be kept strong. We can analyse the benefits of this feature under two main headings:

• improving documentation

• improving user control.

In computer systems documentation of the model is usually good but documentation of the computer code is frequently poor and the links between the model and the code are often absent. The standard of documentation influences the ability to revise or extend the computer system. It is a common experience in business to find that updating a computer system is bewilderingly expensive and sometimes requires a complete rewrite of the code. This is because it is often impossible to determine where revisions in the code should be made or where to add the extra functionality.

When the links between the model and the code are lost it is impossible for the user and the analyst to assess whether the system is truly compatible with their original intentions. In this situation the user can only be involved at the beginning of the development cycle, and critical decisions taken at later stages of development, which might best be taken by the user, are made by programmers. These decisions may be based on assumptions the programmer has made with little or no understanding of the domain that the computer system is expected to serve. This issue is of particular relevance to medicine, which is an extremely complex domain and one of which most people have had only limited experience as patients. Incorrect assumptions made by programmers are the most common source of misunderstanding between clinicians and patients. Maintaining a direct link between the model and the code gives the user control of the later stages of the development cycle and allows the user to make decisions in areas where domain expertise is more relevant than technical expertise.

Object-oriented analysis techniques are supported by object-oriented programming languages. The links in the so-called object-oriented paradigm are much closer than in traditional computer development methodologies. The difference between object-oriented languages and traditional programming languages is that the former encapsulates process with data and the latter separates process from data. Separation of data and code leads to a complicated network of data access and procedural computer code that is difficult to document. The data components in traditional languages are elementary; they include strings (e.g. 'this is a string'), numbers, dates and booleans (i.e. true and false). In contrast, the data components in object-oriented languages are much richer and are defined by the analytical model; thus, in a medical system the data components might be patients, operations and clinics.

Encapsulation of data and process is an extremely powerful principle because it allows the computer system developer to build up applications from discrete modules of code, like a child building a house from Lego bricks. Each concept from the data model is implemented in the code as a *class*. The class determines the relationships and behaviour of all the class members – *objects*. Access to the data held by objects and manipulation of such data can only be made through the computer processes (called *methods*) defined for that class. An object can be visualized as a black box with a series of buttons on the outside (defined by the object's class), which are the object's interface with the outside world (Figure 2.7). In order to access the data within the black box the appropriate button must be pressed. If the data within the box must be changed then other buttons should be pressed, but for each black box the number of buttons on the outside determines the repertoire of manipulations that can be effected. Carefully defined class definitions and their implementations in code as classes can be stored in a class library and reused in other applications that require the same data components. For instance, a patient class might be created for a gastroenterology system and could be reused in a surgical system (Figure 2.8). This modular development and reuse cannot be achieved in traditional programming languages where process and data are created separately but become inextricably linked within the application.

Modular code has another important advantage during the development stage; debugging of coding errors is very much easier when the code can be

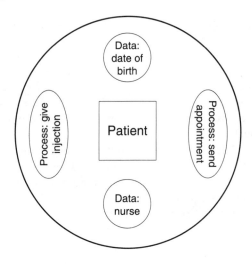

Figure 2.7   Encapsulation of data and process.

logically divided into small, well-documented segments. Extrapolating from this, there is a long-term advantage when modular code is reused in that each module that is reused from a class library will have been tried and tested in previous applications.

Analysis models can be created using software applications called CASE tools (computer-assisted software engineering). At their most primitive level these tools are sophisticated graphics applications for presenting and

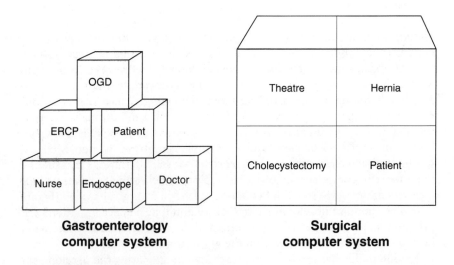

Figure 2.8   Building incremental systems with modular code.

documenting the model. At the next level of sophistication these tools provide a prototyping environment for testing the model with sample data. At their most sophisticated, these tools can be used for generating computer application code directly from analytical models. At this level of sophistication the model is linked to the code and the documentation is complete. Unfortunately, confidence in computer-generated code is not yet at a level at which case tools have become widely accepted, but this is clearly the route for system development in the not too distant future.

Object-oriented analysis and health care

Some benefits of object-oriented technology[1]

Object-oriented analysis allows a new way of looking at old problems. As we have seen object-oriented techniques change information system analysts' view of the world. Instead of thinking about processes and desegregation of processes, they think about objects and their behaviour. The objects may be complex internally, like an electronic machine, but analysts do not need to understand that complexity (unless they design the machine). Knowing how the objects behave and how to use them is enough. This means that the designer thinks in terms of behaviour of objects, not low-level detail. Encapsulation hides the details and makes complex classes easy to use. Classes are like black boxes; developers use the black box and do not look inside it. They have to understand the behaviour of the black box and how to communicate with it. There is also better communication between information system professionals and business people. Business people more easily understand the object-oriented paradigm. They think in terms of events, objects and business policies that describe the behaviour of objects.

The clinical process model,[2] which uses object-oriented methodology, provides a model of the process of health care in object-oriented terms. As we have discussed earlier, emphasis is being placed more and more upon the outcomes that result from a health care intervention.

Drawing upon these sources it is possible to derive a 'black box'[3] approach to health care, whereby the focus is upon the outcome of a health-related intervention rather than the structure or process relating to that intervention. It is therefore worth considering how this technique can be used for health care planning.

The consultation is the currency of clinical medicine. When, for instance, a patient with ischaemic heart disease presents to a physician some or all of the actions shown in Table 2.1 occur.

Table 2.1 Patient presenting with ischaemic heart disease

Action	Outcome
History taking	List and pattern of symptoms
Examination	List and pattern of physical signs
Chest radiograph	Report on the anatomy/pathology of the heart and lung
ECHO cardiogram	Report on the dynamic functions of the heart (including valvular function)
Exercise electrocardiogram	Report on the dynamic function of the heart (including coronary artery function)

'Black boxes'

Each of these stages can be thought of as a black box. Each requires differ-ent skills to perform and to achieve the desired outcome. All clinicians, while not necessarily being able to understand or perform the *process*, e.g. take a chest radiograph, would be able to utilize the information as presented – the outcome.

Consider a lay example of the black box, the videorecorder[3] (Table 2.2). Many families within the UK own and use a videorecorder. They understand that one of its purposes is to record programmes onto blank videotapes (number three in Table 2.2). It is also understood that, in order to record onto a blank tape, the machine will require programming to allow the remote recording of a transmission. This is a task that is carried out with more or less success but, nevertheless, many people in this country have learnt the skills that are required to record the desired programmes successfully.

Table 2.2 Example of the black box: the videorecorder

Action	Outcome
1 Switching on and tuning	Watching television
2 Hiring prerecorded video	Watching film
3 Setting timer and recording	'Time shifting'

The outcome of the process – to videotape and to watch programmes subsequently – can be achieved without knowing how the machine actually converts television signals onto magnetic tape. This is true of many of the black boxes that surround us in everyday life. We have learnt how to use them, but have only the most rudimentary knowledge of their internal workings.

How is this relevant to the provision of health care today, in terms of black boxes? We would propose the following definitions:

• *a provider* is a clinician who understands the process(es) of a black box and can therefore deliver the desired outcome(s) from the black box itself

- *a purchaser* is a clinician who can understand and therefore utilize the outcome(s) of a black box to attain another outcome.

Clinical care as 'black boxes'

While black boxes can be used in isolation, they are destined to become increasingly incorporated into clinical guidelines. There are many different views of clinical guidelines – why they have evolved and to what use they should be put.

Eddy[4] feels that there is wide variation in the beliefs of specialists about the outcomes of given clinical situations and that the development of guidelines means that:

> ... one of the major assumptions underlying the practice of medicine is being challenged. This concerns the intellectual foundation of medical care. Simply put, the assumption is that whatever a physician decides is, by definition, correct. The challenge says that while many decisions are no doubt correct, many are not, and elaborate mechanisms are needed to decide which are which.

Farmer[5] states that clinical guidelines:

> ... have been devised by many different groups, often with differing aims. Some aim to reduce variation in care by using guidelines, while others seek to improve outcomes ... In particular, it is often hard to get guidelines adopted in practice; guidelines must not be unrealistic – those devised by senior doctors away from the realities of day to day practice are likely to fail ... one of the characteristics that has marked the development of clinical standards is the involvement of academics and senior members of the profession. These individuals are sometimes insulated from day to day pressures. Unless a guideline accurately reflects the working practice of most doctors, it will act only as a gold standard to be admired. Rather, it should be an explanation of unsatisfactory practices, a plea for better co-ordination, and a blue-print for simple measures to improve the state of affairs. Perhaps doctors need to be less idealistic and more honest about their present working conditions in order to describe the guidelines to which their practice conforms.

The authors' definition of *clinical guidelines* is as follows: the sum of the black boxes that are required to provide care to a defined standard. It also follows from this that *clinical effectiveness* is the ability of a clinician to provide or purchase appropriate black boxes, to meet given guidelines.

While we feel that the adoption of this approach to guidelines would be beneficial, it is important to sound a note of caution to the wholesale adoption of guidelines, especially by health commissioners. Feder[6] gives a balanced view of the benefits and problems that are associated with guidelines.

Benefits

- guidelines based on the systematically analysed results of research and carefully introduced to doctors can improve clinical practice and outcomes.

Possible disadvantages

- we lack adequate research to make judgements about cost-effectiveness

- only patients care exclusively about clinical outcomes as opposed to costs and outcomes[7]

- guidelines are too weak to bear decisions about allocation of resources

- guidelines are being put forward as a basis for shifting the purchase of health care away from activity towards protocols of care[8]

- in most clinical areas their translation into rigid, enforceable standards of quality would be foolish.[9]

Let us consider a common condition for which clinical guidelines have been issued. If we accept Farmer's[5] argument that clinical guidelines should be implementable rather than seen only as gold standards, we need to draw up a table of essential black boxes that in total represent acceptable clinical care for the group of patients in question.

Benign prostatic hypertrophy

Most men who live long enough will develop benign prostatic hypertrophy.[10] The following tables and text are an example of a set of guidelines set out for the assessment and management of patients with this condition.

Assessment of patients[11]

History   Take a detailed history, including the use of questionnaires.

	Yes	No
Do you think you have difficulty in starting to pass urine?		
Do you think that it takes too long to pass urine?		
Do you pass urine in fits and starts?		
Do you continue to dribble without your full control when you have tried to stop?		
Are you woken from sleep more than twice per night by the need to pass urine?		
Do you sometimes have to rush to the toilet to pass urine?		

A positive response to one or two or more questions indicates the need to pursue a more detailed history. A similar approach is advocated[12] with a more detailed questionnaire – the international prostate symptom score (I–PSS).

	Not at all	Less than 1 time in 5	Less than half the time	About half the time	More than half the time	Almost always
1 Over the past month, how often have you had a sensation of not emptying your bladder completely after you finished urinating?	0	1	2	3	4	5
2 Over the past month, how often have you had to urinate again less than two hours after you finished urinating?	0	1	2	3	4	5
3 Over the past month, how often have you found you stopped and started again several times when you urinated?	0	1	2	3	4	5
4 Over the past month, how often have you found it difficult to postpone urination?	0	1	2	3	4	5
5 Over the past month, how often have you had a weak urinary stream?	0	1	2	3	4	5
6 Over the past month, how often have you had to push or strain to begin urination?	0	1	2	3	4	5
7 Over the past month, how many times did you typically get up to urinate from the time you went to bed at night until the time you got up in the morning?	0	1	2	3	4	5

The total I-PSS score can vary from 0 to 35. No standard cut-off levels have yet been defined, but tentative classification is as follows:

0–7   mildly symptomatic

8–19   moderately symptomatic

20–35   severely symptomatic.

Digital rectal examination (DRE)   An advanced carcinoma causing symptoms would be readily detectable on digital rectal examination.

Creatinine and prostate-specific antigen (PSA) levels   Creatinine allows an assessment of renal function, as long-standing prostatic outflow obstruction can cause renal failure. Prostate-specific antigen is elevated in most patients with significant carcinoma of the prostate.

KUB (kidneys, ureter and bladder radiography) and renal/bladder ultrasound   Plain radiography (KUB) excludes the presence of renal tract stone disease and bony metastatic carcinoma of the prostate. Ultrasound scanning excludes upper-tract dilatation and accurately assesses post-micturition bladder volume.

Measure of urine flow rate   Urine flow rates allow comparison of a patient's maximum flow rate with that of other men of the same age or changes in the same man over time.

Indications for referral
The following are indications for referral:

- malignant-feeling prostate on digital rectal examination

- elevated creatinine

- elevated prostate-specific antigen

- renal stones or metastatic disease

- severe obstruction (flow rate).

Implementing a clinical service
How does this fit in with the provision of a clinical service that requires shared care across the primary/secondary care interface, especially in light of the fact that the merging of the district health authorities and FHSAs into single Joint Commissioning Agencies (JCAs) means that many JCAs are currently looking at the issues surrounding shifting responsibility for the less technological aspects of hospital care into the community?[13]

Our definition of *clinical efficiency* is the ability of a team member to provide or purchase appropriate black boxes, to meet given clinical guidelines, in the most cost-effective manner.

Table 2.3   The role of the health care practitioner

Black box	HCP	Establishment	Outcome
History	GP	Surgery	Establish need for further care
Questionnaire	Nurse (or patient!)	Surgery	Assess symptoms; baseline and ongoing comparison
DRE	GP	Surgery	Refer if feels malignant
PSA and creatinine	Phlebotomist Courier Biochemist	Surgery Hospital	Refer if either is elevated
KUB	Radiographer Radiologist	Hospital	Refer if renal stones or metastases demonstrated
Ultrasound	Radiologist Urologist	Hospital	Refer if flow pattern is abnormal

We must therefore, consider cost-effectiveness. While money is an important measure, we must not lose sight of time, location of service etc. as other indices that need to be taken into account when attempting to measure cost-effectiveness.

In the management of benign prostatic hypertrophy the essential black boxes have to be separated into those that can be provided by general practitioners or their teams and those which must be bought in from the secondary care sector.

As we have seen, in order to provide a black box, at least one team member must possess the necessary skills. What should be organized when more than one member of the team possesses the requisite skills to provide the black box?

The accountabilities that are initially set up are:

- general practitioner and patient

- general practitioner and staff (employed or attached).

The dictionary definition of delegation is 'to commit authority to representatives'. Choosing which team member should provide a black box should also consider the opportunity cost – what else could the health care professional be doing if the black box were being provided by another team member?

The clinically effective general practitioner will organize the care of patients presenting with symptoms suggestive of benign prostatic hypertrophy as shown in Table 2.3.

The division by the GP of black boxes into those which he can provide and those that he will have to purchase can be decided with his secondary care colleagues long before the next patient is seen!

Remember, medical treatment does not in itself require referral to a urologist, providing the GP is willing and able to assess and diagnose the patient's condition.[11]

References

1 Martin J, Odell J (1992) *Object Oriented Analysis and Design*. Prentice Hall, New Jersey.

2 NHS Management Executive-IMG (1992) *The Clinical View of the Common Basic Specification. The Cosmos Project Clinical Process Model Version 2.0*. NHS Management Executive, Birmingham.

3 Edwards P, Jones S, Williams S (1994) *Business and Health Planning for General Practice*, pp. 120–121. Radcliffe Medical Press, Oxford.

4 Eddy D M (1990) Clinical decision making: from theory to practice. The challenge. *JAMA* **263**, 287–290.

5 Farmer A (1993) Medical practice guidelines: lessons from the United States. *Br Med J* **307**, 313–317.

6 Feder G (1994) Clinical guidelines in 1994. *Br Med J* **309**, 1457–1458.

7 Woolf S H (1993) Practice guidelines: a new reality in medicine. III. Impact on patient care. *Arch Intern Med* **153**, 2646–2655.

8 Sheldon T, Browitz M (1993) Changing the measure of quality in the NHS; from purchasing activity to purchasing protocols. *Quality in Health Care* **2**, 149–150.

9 Kassirrer J P (1993) The quality of care and the quality of measuring it. *N Engl J Med* **329**, 1263–1265.

10 Berry S J, Coffey D S, Walsh P C *et al*. (1984) The development of human benign prostatic hyperplasia with age. *J Urol* **132**, 474.

11 Prostate Forum (1994) *BPH in General Practice – An Introduction*. England.

12 *Proceedings of the Second International Consultation on Benign Prostate Hypertrophy, Paris, 1993*.

13 Belsey J (1994) Interface audit and the shift of care. *Managing Audit in General Practice* **2**(4), 6.

3

A flow process model for clinical management of shared care

Consultation, interface audit and total quality management

There is a strong and rich tradition of analysis of the consultation within primary care in the UK. From Byrne and Long,[1] through Scott and Davis[2] and Pendleton et al.[3] to Neighbour,[4] much attention has been focused on this interaction between clinicians and patients. Questions that have been posed include:

- is the patient satisfied with the outcome of the consultation?

- has the doctor made best use of the opportunities available?

- will the general practitioner of the future be able to deal with increasing consumerism?

These have shaped our view of today's 'currency' of clinical care.

One of the consequences of the NHS reforms of the 1990s has been the attempt to persuade clinicians to adopt a 'business culture'. There has been emphasis upon audit – considered as structure, process and outcome. The concept that many clinicians have struggled with is the idea that there is a 'product' as a result of their work. Terms such as 'clinical effectiveness' and 'health gain' have been coined in an attempt to address such tensions.

It should not be forgotten that all clinicians share a common feature in that they invariably are involved in face-to-face contact with patients – they consult. From the patient's viewpoint, their 'health career' consists of a series of consultations with a variety of health care professionals. This describes the process of health care however that health care is organized.

The authors believe that it is possible to construct a flow chart that summarizes the health career of a patient. The flow chart describes a series of processes and outcomes that are applicable to primary and secondary care in a generic manner – both in the specialty of secondary care and also in the health care delivery system (be this in Europe, USA or elsewhere). The flow chart is proposed as a management model, as both clinical and non-clinical aspects of care are encompassed within it.

The model (Figure 3.1) that is described is the result of close clinical collaboration between a general practitioner and hospital consultant (as representatives of primary and secondary care within the NHS) following a close examination of their current clinical practice(s), and the perceived deficiencies therein. Implementation of the model will permit prospective audit of the interface between primary and secondary care, thereby allowing meaningful comparisons of standards and guidelines.[5]

Effective interface audit that involves GPs and hospital doctors and improves patient care is rare. The different organizational cultures of GPs and hospital doctors promote suspicion, impede communication and are thought to contribute to the lack of progress.

In Baker's[5] opinion, interface audit has virtually never taken place, whereas there are numerous examples of specialists investigating the services provided by GPs and vice versa. He has found no examples of a complete audit cycle that included the stages of change and re-evaluation. Audit across the interface will not work if 'finger pointing and laying blame is endemic'. Further progress is unlikely until GPs and consultants are able to understand each other's viewpoints and wishes.

One definition of effective interface audit is 'complete audit cycles conducted by professionals from both primary and secondary care working together as teams to improve quality'.

Interface audit is often promoted as one way to improve cooperation between hospitals and general practice. However, there is neither an accepted definition of what constitutes interface audit nor an identifiable effective methodology. There is little evidence of the lessons of total quality management (TQM)[6] being understood.

Total quality management is a way of managing to improve the effectiveness, flexibility and competitiveness of a business as a whole. Specific characteristics include:

- management leadership focused on quality
- continuous effort to improve quality
- a focus on the customer's definition of quality
- avoidance of 'finger pointing' or blaming outside groups for problems.

The contracts between purchaser and provider have introduced the concept of the customer, but this has yet to become established in the minds of the clinicians.

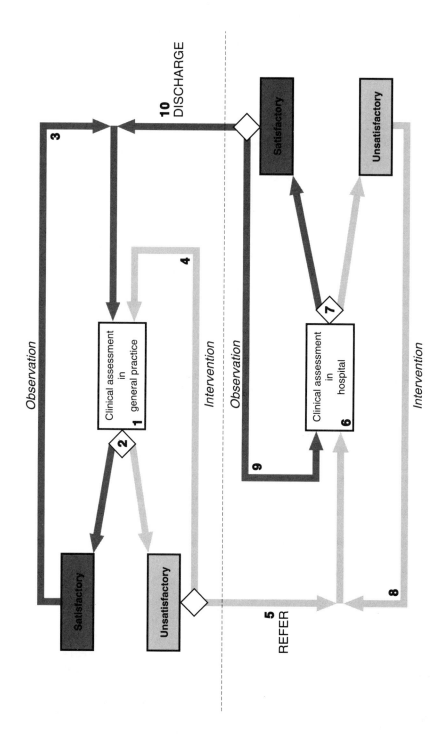

Figure 3.1 The flow process model of clinical management.

Effective audit is unlikely until GPs and specialists are able to understand the viewpoints and wishes of each other. They need to know how the health service looks from each other's perspective.

The flow process model[7] more commonly found in industrial settings offers an approach to interface audit. It provides a framework for examining the service from the patient's point of view, with each stage of care broken down into steps. The problems that a patient may encounter at each stage are identified, studied and resolved. It is this emphasis on the patient's perspective that makes flow process audit particularly valuable.

Effective audit across organizational barriers has proved elusive. The solution to improve the value of interface audit depends upon improved relationships across the interface. In its most complete form this would be equivalent to teamwork. In ideal circumstances GPs and specialists would then learn from each other how to modify their performance in order to meet the requirements of their 'internal customers'.

The author's model is best exemplified by application to discrete clinical areas such as asthma, angina and benign prostatic hypertrophy, yet is applicable to both acute and chronic care. It can be viewed from many angles – the role of the primary care doctor or nurse, the secondary care doctor or nurse. One of its main strengths however is that it can be applied to patients throughout their health care career – an effective adaptation of flow process audit.

Describing a flow process model for shared care

The authors feel that the applicability of the flow process model presented in Figure 3.1 is such that it can be considered a generic representation of shared care across all specialties. In all areas of activity, such as acute or chronic care in medical and surgical specialties, there needs to be fine tuning to meet the individual needs of patients in clinical or disease groups. In essence, the distinction between primary and secondary care is false in that the processes of activity are essentially a mirror image of activity.

The consultation – primary and secondary care

There is no difference in the process of consultation between care sectors (**1** and **6**). Consultation is the primary currency of clinical medicine. During this process an accountability is set up between the patient and doctor, both long-term and on each occasion when the patient and doctor meet. The kernel of the consultation process consists in a series of observations regarding patients and their state of health. Observations may be either subjective or objective, and in a shared care model as proposed here they may be made either by the patient or by the doctor. Through this approach patients' input at the level of first consultation with either the primary or secondary care physician becomes paramount and empowers the patient with regard to decision making.

Decision making

In the shared care model presented here the process of decision making (2 and 7) is the same either side of the primary and secondary interface. In each sector the clinical process leads to the synthesis of a mutually exclusive state of satisfactory or unsatisfactory. The decision as to which state exists is made by the patient and the doctor involved, with reference to accepted standards and agreed outcomes. Standards selected can be subjective or objective in nature and may be explicit or implicit in the process of clinical assessment. In practical terms those standards may be evidence-based, guideline-based and adopted by medical staff. Patients' standards may be based upon their individual quality of life and perception of what is required.

Observation

This occurs in both primary and secondary care (3 and 9) but is essentially, in a shared care model, the role of primary care. It may be a passive process in which the patient and clinician agree that the health status is satisfactory and that the patient can be observed over a period of time. At this point both the patient and the doctor take responsibility for making the clinical assessment. In addition, both the patient and the doctor can make a decision as to how long the watching process should continue. This decision may be arrived at conventionally, the patient being given a fixed time period to the next appointment, or the patient may be allowed to decide when review is necessary because of deterioration. With such a system it may be possible to set specific explicit standards; for example, three assessments that are satisfactory might lead to a reduction in medication in primary care or to the patient being transferred automatically from secondary to primary care.

Intervention

This is an active process in which a number of interventions can be made by the primary (4 or 5) or secondary care (8) clinician for patients deemed to be of unsatisfactory health status. Such patients may be reassessed frequently because of an earlier assessment made by the patient and the doctor of progression of the underlying pathology. The reasons for this alteration in the period of observation may involve further investigations, such as blood tests, sputum culture or radiographic investigations. The patient may also be seen frequently in an attempt to check compliance with medication and/or to assess the impact of altering medication. The latter may involve an increase in dosage, an alteration to a different type of drug or adding further medication to that already being taken. Such changes may involve the patient to a lesser or greater degree depending on the nature of the background problem and the options for self-management. Hence, when the patient is reviewed, an assessment will be made to determine the impact of the interventions that are being made and what further changes need to be made, if any. At this point the patient may re-enter the watching limb if, through the reconsultation, both the patient and clinician reach a decision of 'satisfactory'. In primary care this may lead to a further appointment of a fixed time period, while in secondary care it may lead to a decision of further consultation (9) or referral back to primary care (10).

Routine clinic attendance

This is the locus at which the clinician and patient agree on whether the patient's health status is satisfactory or not. When a satisfactory state is agreed upon the patient enters a loop of observation (3 or 9). Here the patient takes responsibility for making further clinical assessments until they are reviewed by the health professional. In either primary or secondary care this may involve measurements at home, e.g. blood glucose or peak expiratory flow rates, and possibly some form of response to changes in these measures. This may be part of a self-management plan leading to an increase in insulin or an increase in corticosteroid treatment in asthma. A further aspect of such self-management is that the patient can be given specific objective measures of when further medical help is obtained or can wait until the planned return to clinic. In the latter case the patient is reviewed after a set period of time because of the stability of clinical status. In an ideal system, deterioration in the patient's clinical status will result in an earlier review and changes to medication made in the form of an intervention.

In the setting of secondary care there is often a routine arrangement of repeated review without a specific management plan. Patients therefore may attend outpatients for many years on a regular basis with no real mechanism of escape from the system. This is partly the result of patient choice and partly due to the pattern of training of junior staff in secondary care, in which decision making is not necessarily encouraged and patients are given further appointments without real purpose.

A patient whose clinical status becomes unsatisfactory is usually assessed in the primary care sector on the clear understanding that the patient can, if appropriate, be referred to the secondary care sector. This process is sometimes circumvented in the case of patients with known severe disease, who may have direct access to secondary care via an open door policy. The latter approach requires agreement between three parties: the patient, the primary care physician and the secondary care physician. As the development of a shared care plan for an individual patient evolves then all three parties need to agree on shifts of emphasis in the care of the patient between primary and secondary care.

Transfer of care

It is the responsibility of the primary clinician to decide whether the resources available are insufficient to provide the standard of agreed management for a given patient. If so, the patient's care is transferred to the secondary care sector (5). Ideally, the patient's explicit needs are communicated to the consultant, in either the acute or non-urgent referral setting. The referral should be based on the patient's perception of need in addition to that of the primary care physician.

The secondary care clinician must decide whether the resources of the primary care team are adequate to allow the patient's transfer back to primary care (10). Currently this is something of a 'lottery', as is evident by the differences in practice between different consultants in the same hospital and between consultants in different hospitals. Coordination of discharge into the community is an area requiring improvement in terms of clinical effectiveness and outcomes for the patient. This can be achieved in the setting of shared care by the development of joint standards of care, which are not widely used currently but provide for the location of care being less important than the standard of care. This allows patients to rapidly return to care in the community following referral to secondary care.

Shared care – the future

The operational model at a clinical level provides a mechanism for the transfer of care between primary and secondary care and regulation of activity within a given shared care grouping. For this process to function effectively it is imperative that both the primary and secondary care clinicians derive common standards of care and a pattern of review of patients. Patients and health care professionals other than medical staff should be involved in the derivation of these standards.

Providing that specialist equipment is not required it should be possible to ensure that appropriate assessment can take place at any location to the same standard of care. There is therefore no reason why patients should attend hospital outpatients on a regular basis for simple review. The locus of their care becomes much less important if common standards can be agreed.·

The patient who is deemed satisfactory in secondary care can be discharged to primary care. In the setting of the shared care system patients can be reviewed to the same standards that exist in secondary care.

Implementation of the model will ensure that patients with severe but stable disease will be looked after in primary care – their assessment will be satisfactory in regard to the standards of care set and their own assessment of their condition. However, those with unstable or fluctuating disease status will often not be considered satisfactory by either themselves or their primary care physician and can be referred to secondary care. Those who are unsatisfactory and require intervention will therefore see the doctor with regard to active management. Those who are satisfactory and whose treatment can be maintained or reduced, i.e. who require a passive approach, can be viewed by either the doctor or the nurse, which would allow patients to be transferred from primary to secondary care or secondary back to primary care by liaison between nurses in each care sector.

Restructuring the model in object-oriented terms

The flow process model presented above has allowed an examination of the flow of patients between primary and secondary care. A number of issues influencing this process required effort to translate the flow process model to an object-oriented model that is compatible with the Cosmos Clinical Process Model (which is an object-oriented model of health care as a whole). The method used to devise the object-oriented model is described in Chapter 4. Interestingly, the translation to a more rigorous modelling technique was in itself beneficial as it enforced a more thorough definition of what constitutes satisfactory and unsatisfactory.

The Cosmos Clinical Process Model provides a structural framework of the clinical domain, and the model of shared care is a dynamic view of the processes that impact on the concepts of that model. Thus the shared care model is described by using an event diagram, and each event described modifies the attributes of concepts in the clinical process model.

References

1 Byrne P, Long B (1976) *Doctors Talking to Patients*. HMSO, London.

2 Stott N C H, Davis R H (1979) The exceptional potential in each primary care consultation. *J Roy Coll Gen Pract* **29**, 201–205.

3 Pendleton D, Schofield T, Tate P (1984) *The Consultation. An Approach to Learning Teaching*. Oxford University Press, Oxford.

4 Neighbour R (1987) *The Inner Consultation*. MTP Press, Lancaster.

5 Baker R (1994) What is interface audit? *J R Soc Med* **87**, 228–231.

6 Oakland J (1990) *Total Quality Management: A Practical Approach*. Department of Trade and Industry, London.

7 Ovretveit J (1992) *Health Services Quality*. Blackwell Special Products, Oxford.

4

An object-oriented approach to modelling health care

Models used in the NHS

The National Health Service, as the largest such organization in Europe, generates an enormous amount of data. Inevitably, a large proportion of the data are redundant and the critical information tends to get lost among the bulk. In the early 1980s it was recognized that certain types of data should be saved prospectively for use in NHS management. The first attempts to organize the data generated by health care were made by consensus groups brought together as the Koerner committees. These committees produced six reports that recommended the use of specific data sets for use in the local management of district health authorities including hospitals and community units.

Recognizing the need to provide structure for the health care data, the NHS Computer Policy Unit commissioned a feasibility study from the management consultants Arthur Andersen to assess the benefit of data modelling. The report of this feasibility study led to the inception of the Corporate Data Administration, whose first task was to document the Koerner committee reports as a data model using a formal notation. The result of this project became the NHS Minimum Data Set Model, which was subsequently incorporated in the NHS Data Dictionary. The Data Dictionary is still widely used in NHS administration and is maintained by the Committee for Regulating Information Requirements.

The second project undertaken by the Corporate Data Administration was creation of the NHS Data Model. This project drew on the experiences of a large number of computer systems development teams within the NHS, and its results were published in 1987.

In 1988 the NHS Management Board (now replaced by the NHS Management Executive) approved a programme to develop a common basis for the specification (CBS) of computer systems for use within the NHS. This programme lasted four years and consumed a budget of £7.4 million. More than 30 projects contributed to the models that were finally published. Among these were three clinically led projects based in diverse clinical specialties:

1   paediatrics at The Hospital for Sick Children, Great Ormond Street

2   diabetes at St Thomas' Hospital

3   organ transplantation at St Mary's Hospital.

The results of these clinical modelling efforts were inevitably found to have a high degree of commonality, and thus the Cosmos Project at St Mary's was commissioned to develop a generic model of clinical medicine – published in 1992 as *The Cosmos Clinical Process Model: The Clinical View of The Common Basic Specification.*[1] Two further published models were produced by the CBS programme: the *CBS Generic Model*[2] and the *Public Health Information Specification.*

Following on from the modelling phase of the CBS programme, a demonstration phase was instituted in which four self-funded demonstrator projects used the CBS models to develop health care information systems. These projects were overseen by an assessment board made up of representatives of the Royal Colleges, industry, NHS management and academia. The CBS Assessment Board has now completed its work and is preparing a report for the Management Executive.

The Cosmos Project, although commissioned only to develop a model of health care, managed to complete some initial testing of the clinical model by developing a computer prototype. This prototype was developed to serve the needs of a transplant immunology department involved in donor–recipient matching. This prototype has proved successful in holding an electronic medical record as it pertains to this specialized area of medicine and has also shown that the data model is sufficiently extensive to sustain a decision support application.

The Cosmos Model now forms the basis of a new application for storing clinical, laboratory and molecular biology data on patients treated for viral hepatitis in a London teaching hospital. In Wales the model is being used as a basis for developing a computer system to support the shared care of asthma patients, and in the USA the model is being used for the diagnosis and treatment of financial problems in a large multinational company!

Shared care is a clinical process which has its own specific pattern of behaviour. The conceptual model underlying shared care does not differ from the model underlying any other clinical process in as much as it still deals in patients, procedures, clinical observations etc. However, as dynamic behaviour in shared care differs from that in more traditional referral practice, it is most easily represented with a dynamic model using object-oriented event diagrams. Event diagrams must be linked to a concept diagram showing the structure and relationships of the objects whose state changes in the dynamic model. *The Cosmos Clinical Process Model* is a generic concept diagram catering for all aspects of clinical practice. The model of shared care developed by the authors is underpinned by the Cosmos Model and therefore a full description of this conceptual model is initially discussed.

The Cosmos Clinical Process Model

A common model of health care, as with other models, provides a vehicle for communication between clinicians from all areas of medicine and for the planners and managers of health care services. A common model is therefore a tool that can be used to negotiate the interfaces between primary and secondary care and to specify the contracts between purchasers and providers of care. When the common model is implemented in clinical computer applications it provides a data structure through which data may be shared by disparate clinical systems. When clinical computer applications are built using a custom rather than common data model, problems occur when attempts are made to integrate the data. An example of such problems occurred in a hospital department in which independent databases had been created to handle clinical information generated by a multitude of clinical drug trials. Despite using the same database tool there is no easy procedure for transferring data from one data set to another, nor can the data be readily integrated as the data structures are critically different.

A common model is achieved through exclusion of fine detail and abstraction of critical concepts from all areas of the relevant domain. The process of abstraction has a drawback in that it takes the model a step further away from the real world that it strives to represent. In the model described below, in which the objective is to represent the entire domain of clinical care, there is inevitably a high degree of abstraction which means that some concepts, such as diagnosis, are not immediately perceived by the casual observer. In developing such a model there are two opposing pressures on the modellers:

- the need to represent all areas of the clinical domain demands a high level of abstraction
- the need for the model to be comprehensible without extensive tuition demands a low level of abstraction.

Through experience in presenting this model to a wide range of audiences from both clinical and computer science backgrounds, the authors realize that the naming of some concepts results in confusion or misinterpretation. This partly results from the ability in natural language to be loose about the definition of terms. However, in a formal modelling technique concepts must be formally defined so that confusion does not occur.

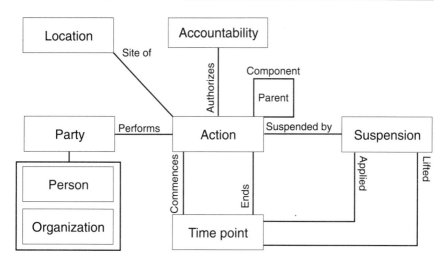

Figure 4.1   Clinical actions.

Object-oriented models represent the real world from two perspectives:

- the structural schema is used to represent the key objects in the real world and the relationships between them, e.g. patients are the focus of clinical procedures and the procedures use up resources

- the dynamic schema describes how objects and their relationships change over time.

It has been found that the structural schema described below adequately represents the broad range of clinical domains, but it is more difficult to represent dynamic behaviour at a generic level. It is the dynamic behaviour of clinicians and departments that gives them individuality, and therefore representation of dynamic behaviour is not essential to the common model.

Clinical actions (Figure 4.1)

The model of clinical care has been called the clinical process model as it describes the process of health care. It is therefore apt that the description should start with the concept *action*, whose definition is fairly intuitive, apart from the qualification that actions are performed by clinicians and clinicians are people whose professional training is directed towards maintaining/improving health. Actions have *performers*, who may be persons or organizations, and these two concepts are brought together by a unifying concept called *party*. Actions may be made up of any number of component actions, which is represented in the modelling syntax as an iterative relationship on the concept of action. Through this relationship

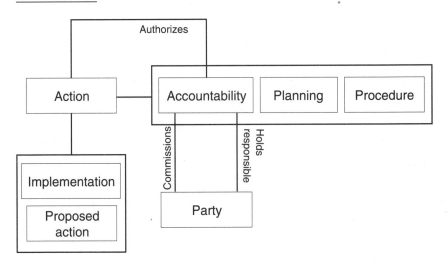

Figure 4.2 Proposed action and implementation.

each component action may inherit the attributes of its parent(s) or be given its own separate attributes. Actions are performed at *locations* and have *time points* that represent their commencement and conclusion. In the clinical domain actions require appropriate authorities before they are performed, such as consent for an operation or, more recently, a purchaser–provider contract. Authority is provided by *accountability*, which represents agreements between two parties, often the patient and a clinician. To cater for the situation where, for instance, an operation is put off owing to the patient's intercurrent infection, an action can be subjected to *suspensions*, which have their own set of time points.

Proposed action and implementation (Figure 4.2)

The concept 'action' is subclassified to allow for the representation of actions that are planned for the future. Thus, actions may be *proposed actions* or *implementations*. The ability to use a subclassification or subtyping relationship in object-oriented modelling is extremely powerful: it allows us to add many layers of detail to the model, but it implies that all members of the subclass inherit the relationships of the superclass. It is possible to subtype a concept on more than one basis, e.g. a person may be male or female but a person can also be a doctor or a nurse. Each subtyping classification creates a separate box on the concept diagram called a partition. Actions may therefore be further subtyped on the basis of the sort of action. This subtyping creates a new partition that includes the concepts *planning*, *accountability* and *procedure*. Planning is fairly self-evident and allows the clinician to coordinate future investigations and therapeutic procedures for the patient. *Accountability* was referred to earlier in the context of giving

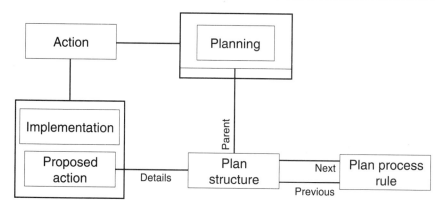

Figure 4.3   Planning.

authority to actions. It may seem odd initially that this concept, basically representing an agreement between two parties, should be a subtype of *action*. However, the essentials of any agreement that is to be represented in the clinical domain are the details of the setting up of the agreements. *Procedures* are the actions enacted on patients and which either observe or attempt to change the patient's state of health.

Planning (Figure 4.3)

Planning generates a set of *proposed actions* that are referenced through *plan structures*. The purpose of the plan is to allow the coordination of *proposed actions* using a set of rules represented by the concept *plan process rules*. Plan process rules create a sequence in which the list of proposed actions should be executed. This process is often performed, to a variable level of competence, by house physicians or surgeons.

Procedure and protocols (Figure 4.4)

Procedures are enacted on *objects of care*, an unwieldy term that allows us to consider either individuals or populations (in the context of public health medicine). *Procedure* is subtyped into *observations* and *interventions*. Observations have been defined as procedures whose principal aim is to observe the state of health of an object of care. An intervention is a procedure that aims to change (or risks changing) the state of health of the object of care. These definitions are helpful therefore in distinguishing a diagnostic endoscopy from a therapeutic endoscopy. However, it can be seen that in both of these procedures the state of health of the patient is clearly changed by the administration of sedatives. Bearing in mind that all actions, and therefore all procedures, may be built up from components, there is a component procedure – sedation – that changes the state of health of the patient

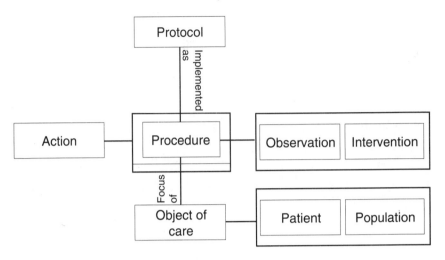

Figure 4.4   Procedure and protocols.

and is therefore an *intervention* even if the aim of the parent action is to observe the state of health of the patient.

In the medical professions *procedures* are rarely just invented and enacted on the spot. In practice, clinicians implement procedures that were learned as part of professional training. This knowledge of how to perform procedures has been called *protocols*. The term protocol occasionally creates misunderstanding, as in some contexts, e.g. chemotherapy regimens or drug trials, protocol is used to represent a formal sequence of clinical actions. This is only one of the meanings which the term is intended to embody.

Knowledge and operational levels (Figure 4.5)

Procedures are considered in the model as the implementations of protocols. This highlights an important feature of the clinical process model – the separation of clinical knowledge from the operational details of clinical practice. In the graphical representation of the model there is a horizontal line approximately midway down the model that divides *knowledge level* concepts from *operational level* concepts. This division has relevance whether the model is being used as the basis for an electronic health record or for negotiating the interfaces between primary and secondary care.

The objects represented by concepts in the knowledge level are provided by bodies of clinical knowledge; thus the complete collection of protocols could be created from a standard thesaurus of coded clinical terms such as OPCS4 (or Read). The objects derived from the operational level are supplied by specific clinical activity and therefore recording clinical events populates the operational level in order to create a clinical record. The clinical record, however, requires references to knowledge level objects to

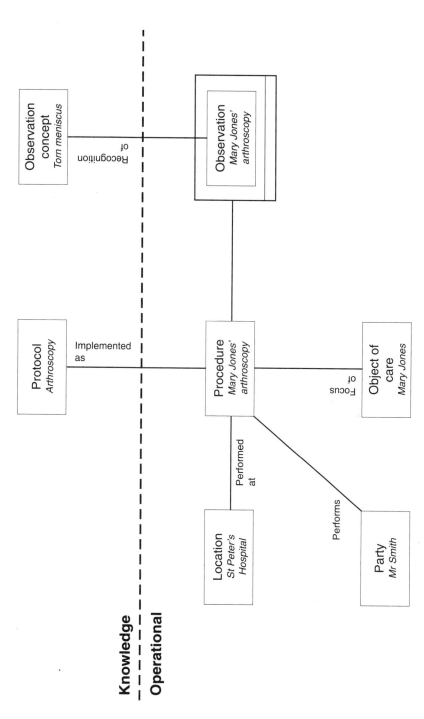

Figure 4.5 Knowledge and operational levels.

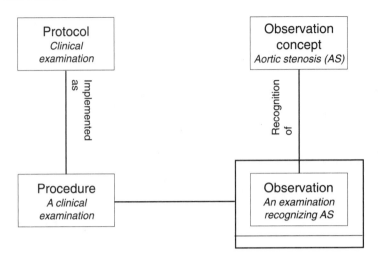

Figure 4.6   Observations.

give it meaning. For example (see Figure 4.5) it is insufficient to say that Mary Jones had a procedure performed by Mr Smith at St Peter's Hospital on 25 January 1995: we actually need a reference to a protocol (e.g. arthroscopy) to give this example sufficient detail and meaning.

Observations (Figure 4.6)

Observations recognize symptoms, signs and conditions. Clinicians recognize what they are taught to recognize, and these can be grouped together as *observation concepts*. When the finding of aortic stenosis is noted on examination this is represented in the model as an observation procedure that used the protocol clinical examination and recognized the observation concept aortic stenosis.

   This may appear to be very long-winded, but it is in reality a more precise representation of what is really meant when the shorthand representation is written in the paper record. Furthermore, if in the future it is necessary to trace the evidence for aortic stenosis it is essential to know that it was a clinical examination rather than a more objective cardiac catheter examination.

Associated observation and diagnosis (Figure 4.7)

Diagnoses are made by considering all the observations made about a patient and comparing those that provide evidence to support a hypothetical diagnosis with those that may refute it. It may be desired to record on a clinical record the observations that were used in support

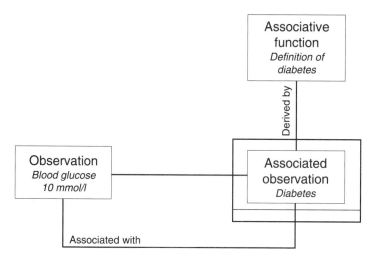

Figure 4.7   Associated observation and diagnosis.

of a diagnosis, and therefore the model has a subtype of observation called associated observation. A simple example of this is the observation of a fasting blood glucose of 10 mmol/l. The links between any two associated observations may take many different forms; in the example given above the fasting blood glucose measurement not only provides evidence for diabetes, it defines diabetes according to the criteria laid down by the World Health Organization. The nature of these associations is part of clinical knowledge and is represented in the model as associative functions. Other associative functions would be the empirical link between ankylosing spondylitis and aortic valve disease or the shared aetiology that links coronary artery disease with cerebrovascular disease.

States of observations (Figure 4.8)

It is difficult to represent certainty of observation, and there is little by way of guidance in the paper record. However, it has been considered useful to distinguish the use to which an observation is put. Thus, when a patient is seen by a clinician a list of differential diagnoses may be made and investigations or further examinations may be planned in order to support or refute each of the diagnoses. Occasionally a patient's condition may be so perilous that action has to be taken before confirmatory tests can be instigated, thus one of the differential diagnoses is used as an argument for an intervention. Any observation used as an argument for an intervention is represented as an *observation* (the working diagnosis) no matter what the level of certainty in the diagnosis, whereas observations that will only

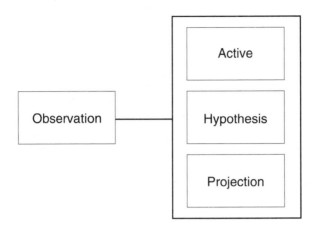

Figure 4.8   States of observation.

be used as an argument for further investigations are represented as hypotheses. Observations may be made about the future state of health of a patient, and these are called projections.

Biological phenomena (Figure 4.9)

Many of the observations made about patients are not about diseases but concern normal variations or polymorphisms such as ethnic background or blood group. It is useful to separate these from other observation concepts by creating a subtype called biological phenomena. Biological phenomenon

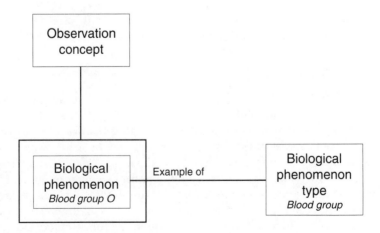

Figure 4.9   Biological phenomena.

types are the broad headings that classify biological phenomena: the relationship between the two concepts is best illustrated by considering the following example. Blood group is the biological phenomenon type for the biological phenomena blood group O, blood group A, blood group B etc. It does not make sense to say that an observation recognizes blood group but it does make sense to recognize blood group O. Biological phenomena are therefore subtypes of observation concepts. Biological phenomenon types may also be physiological variables such as peak expiratory flow rate, which can be given a numerical value. A measurement protocol (a subtype of protocol) should therefore be linked to a biological phenomenon type to explain what is being measured.

Measurements (Figure 4.10)

Many of the tests performed in medicine give numerical results that are handled by a subtype of observation called measurement. Measurements have an attribute called quantity, which itself has attributes number and unit. Measurements implement measurement protocols, and through this relationship the nature of what is being measured (a biological phenomenon type) may be derived. It is possible to specify ranges for clinical values that are bounded by upper or lower limits or both. Thus, the normal range for fasting blood glucose lies between 3.0 and 5.0 mmol/l.

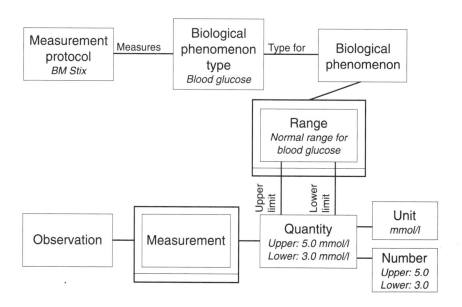

Figure 4.10   Measurements.

Problems and differentials (Figure 4.11)

There are just two further subclassifications of observation to consider. It is useful to be able to represent certain observations as problems in a similar way as the problem-oriented medical record differentiated active and inactive problems.

Certain observations are made as a result of comparing two or more previous observations, for instance asthma may be diagnosed on the peak expiratory flow rates before and after a bronchodilator. This type of observation is represented by a differential, which has relationships to two or more observations.

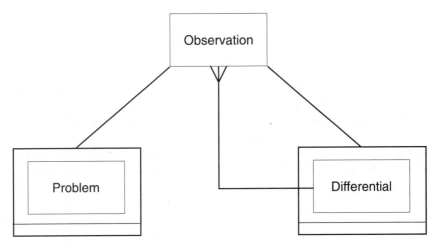

Figure 4.11   Problems and differentials.

Knowledge concepts

Biological phenomenon type and observation concept have been made subtypes of the concept knowledge concept. The principal purpose of this is a modelling technique that allows the addition of some common behaviour to both concepts. Knowledge concepts have an iterative relationship (similar to that on action) with them that permits classification and subclassification: an example might be that type 1 diabetes is a subclass of diabetes or that inflammatory bowel disease classifies Crohn's disease and ulcerative colitis.

Accountability and clinical scope (Figure 4.12)

Accountability is the concept representing the setting up of an agreement between two parties. As it is a subtype of action, we can represent or record

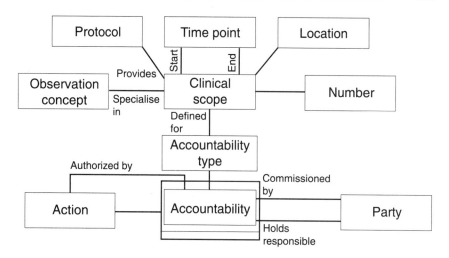

Figure 4.12   Accountability and clinical scope.

the time, place, performers and the components of setting up the account-ability. The nature of the accountability is given by a relationship to the concept accountability type. There may be an enormous number of account-ability types required to represent a clinical domain but the familiar ex-amples will be:

- consent for operation

- employment contract for a consultant with a hospital trust

- contracts between fundholding GP and a hospital trust.

It is clear that some of these cases, particularly contracts, require more detail, which is provided by *clinical scope*. Clinical scope has relationships to observation concept, protocol, number, time points and location so that a contract may specify the type of disease for which a clinician or organiza-tion must provide care, or the type and number of procedures that must be provided. We have not considered the financial details to be part of the clin-ical process, but this information could easily be represented by attributes on protocols or clinical scope.

Resource (Figure 4.13)

The use of *resources* is currently handled in a relatively simplistic way as resource management is not considered a directly clinical activity. A more

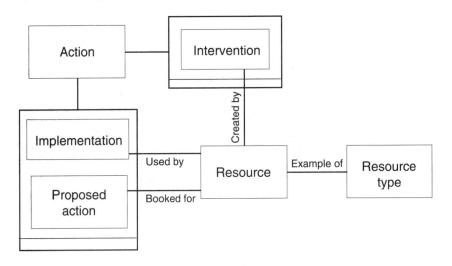

Figure 4.13   Resources.

sophisticated representation is currently under development to handle the ownership of resources, differences between capital and consumable resources and the division of capital resources into time slots. Resources at the operational level are the manifestation of resource types at the knowledge level. Resources may be booked for proposed actions or used by implementations.

The relationship between protocols and resource types tells us which resources are required to perform procedures, which is useful in the planning of clinical services. Some resources, such as blood samples and organs for transplantation, need to be created by clinical procedures, which is represented by a relationship between resource and intervention.

Knowledge functions (Figure 4.14)

Clinical knowledge is not just the knowledge of what procedures can be performed and what can be observed, it is also important to know which observation procedures should be used to recognize specific observation concepts and in which circumstances specific interventions are contraindicated. This role is served by a set of knowledge functions which, by analogy to mathematical functions, take one or more arguments and return a value or set of values:

1   observation function (a subtype of knowledge function) takes as an argument an observation protocol (subtype of protocol) and returns a set of observation concepts that may be recognized by that observation protocol

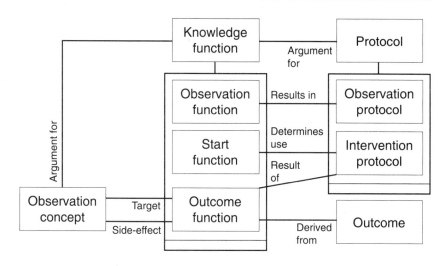

Figure 4.14   Knowledge functions.

2   outcome function takes as an argument an intervention protocol (sub-type of protocol) and returns a set of intended (or target) observation concepts and a set of side-effects – also observation concepts

3   the indications and contraindications for any protocol are given by a start function.

The ability to represent this complex area of clinical practice using object-oriented analysis techniques has facilitated the development of decision support applications.

The flow process model for shared care in object-oriented terms

The authors' model of shared care has already been demonstrated in terms of a flow process diagram, but the diagrammatic constructions used have no formal syntax or meaning. The model conveys the concept to clinicians by exploiting the clinicians' own experience and intuition. When we express the model using the formal notation of the object-oriented event diagram we make the meaning clear to non-clinicians and remove the ambiguity of interpretation that occurs when comprehension is dependent on intuition.

Shared care for a chronic disease, e.g. hypertension, diabetes, asthma cannot be represented as a simple linear event diagram with a clear initiating and a clear goal event. The process is in reality cyclical, with recurrent episodes of assessment, planning, monitoring and therapy. The initiating event is the point at which the diagnosis is made, and the final event occurs when the patient dies. Taking asthma as an example, shared care may also be initiated when a patient with the diagnosis registers with a new GP. Whatever the initiating event the first process which occurs in this management cycle is assessment of the asthma (Figure 4.15).

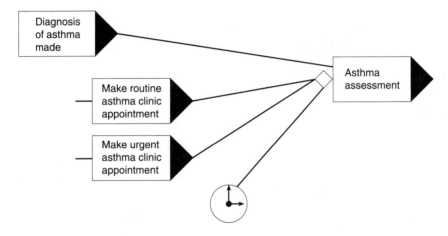

Figure 4.15   Initiating an asthma assessment.

Assessment is a complex action as represented in the concept diagram. This action is performed by the clinician and the patient together and the action is usually going to be the implementation of a proposed action (which represents the scheduling of asthma assessments). The assessment will be made up of the following components (Figure 4.16):

- observation – the history of recent symptoms
- observation – the respiratory examination
- observation – the peak expiratory flow rate (or lung function tests).

As a result of these observations a decision must be made; in the flow process diagram we have shown that the clinical situation may be deemed 'satisfactory' or 'unsatisfactory'. These are loose terms that leave room for some ambiguity, and the event model requires that we give more precise definition to this decision. Clearly the very existence of the asthma is 'unsatisfactory', and in patients with severe disease the asthma may be poorly controlled and disabling. However, if the patient's medication is optimized

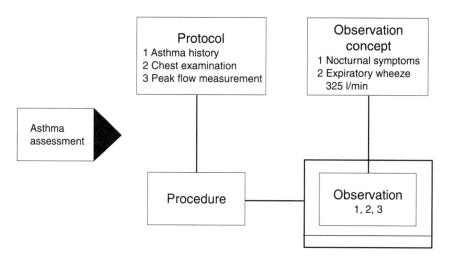

Figure 4.16   Relationship of events to the concept diagram. The asthma assessment event creates several new observations.

and the frequency of review and self-monitoring is adequate, then no changes will be made to the patient's current management. In fact, when the situation is fully analysed the decision of 'satisfactory' or 'unsatisfactory' actually pertains to the current plan of management as opposed to a direct observation about the patient. If the current plan of management is satisfactory then the shared care cycle continues, but if the current plan is unsatisfactory then a subtype of the 'assessment completed' event triggers a planning process (Figure 4.17).

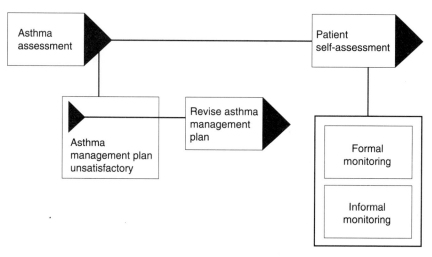

Figure 4.17   Events following asthma assessment.

The trigger for planning will often be that the patient's status has deter-iorated. Thus, in the concept diagram we can draw a link between one of the observations that has just been made and planning. It is hoped that the trigger for planning will in some cases be that the patient has improved sufficiently to reduce medication or to reduce the frequency of assessments. Planning creates a set of proposed actions that represent the details of our shared care asthma management plan. The set of proposed actions may include (Figure 4.18):

- drug treatments

- assessment schedules

- self-monitoring protocols

- transfer to secondary care or return to primary care

- investigations

- immediate admission.

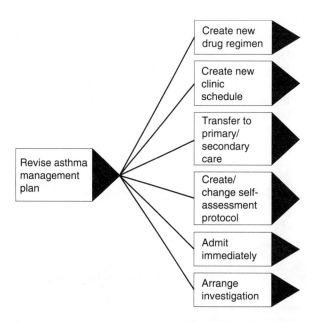

Figure 4.18 Planning triggers the creation of new proposed actions (the details of the plan).

After the assessment process monitoring of disease status is resumed by the patient. This may be an informal process in which the patient only notes deteriorations of symptoms and reports them at the next assessment. Altern-atively, the patient may be given a formal protocol to use in the monitoring of the disease, such as the completion of a peak flow chart. If there is a dramatic change in condition the patient is given leave to arrange an urgent appointment for assessment. If there is no deterioration then a clock operator triggers the next routine appointment (Figure 4.19).

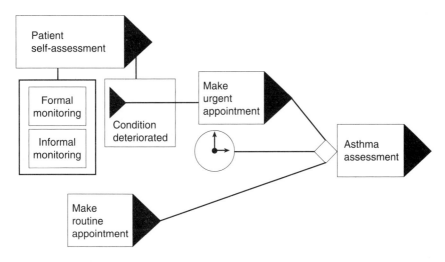

Figure 4.19   Patient monitoring may result in an urgent appointment.

When, as a result of a new management plan, investigation results are received by the clinician, a different type of assessment is triggered. In this case the clinician decides in the light of the new result, and bearing in mind the patient's condition when last assessed, whether the management plan needs to be revised. Thus, although the details of the assessment process are different in this case (represented by a subtype of the assessment process), the subsequent events do not alter (Figure 4.20).

The sequence of events described above is no different whether the patient is seen in primary care or secondary care. The key to shared care is therefore the management plan; it is essential that each of the clinicians involved in the patient's care and the patient, has access to the plan. In order that the plan need not be changed at every assessment, some contingencies should be written into the plan, such as variation in the dose of bronchodilators.

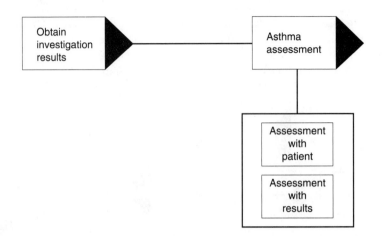

Figure 4.20 Acquiring investigation results triggers a different type of assessment.

References

1 NHS Management Executive (1991) *Integrating Primary and Secondary Health Care* EL (91) 27. Department of Health, London.

2 Rolfe P, Jones D (1992) *The Common Basis Specification*. NHS Information Management Group.

5

Components of one-sector care

Clinical assessment

When, in general practice, a patient signs the registration form FP1 and is accepted on to a general practitioner principal's list, an accountability is set up between the patient and the primary care doctor. The accountability takes the form of an agreement that care will be provided on a continuous basis. The expectations of both parties are based on their view of the historical nature of the general practitioner relationship with patients, as well as the general practitioner's terms of service, the Patient's Charter etc.

The consultation is the usual method of delivery of that care and constitutes the basis of clinical assessment.

When the patient consults for the first time, the doctor will have to rely on history and examination. Within general practice in the NHS, there is no tradition of rapid transfer of written medical records from the patient's previous GP except in exceptional circumstances, in which case the clinician has to make a specific request. Although we live in a computerized age, electronic links have not yet been established to allow instant access to a new patient's existing medical record.

The process of history taking and examination is the substance of the consultation. The outcome of each consultation should be to make a decision as to the state of the patient's health at that point in time. This process will have to be repeated for each problem that is presented, as well as for chronic conditions, health promotion and help-seeking behaviours.[1]

Family physicians tend to ask fewer history questions and request fewer items of physical examination, but overall ask more questions relating to life situation and mental health than their secondary care colleagues.[2,3]

Traditionally, clinical consultation in hospital is seen as being for the benefit of the patient, but the consultation is carried out in a highly regulated way that meets the needs of both clinicians and managers in respect of a rapid throughput of activity. Components of the consultation include:

- gathering of information
- processing of that information

- instigation of a variety of investigations

- implementation of management options

- a review of the impact of the management choices.

This face-to-face contact between clinician and patient allows the collection of subjective and objective information. Experienced clinicians will be able to assess patients' clinical state as well as to allow patients to express their view.

While the general practitioner must frequently diagnose what things are not, rather than what they are, and often must make management decisions before a definitive diagnosis is reached,[4] the hospital physician has to deal with initial consultations with patients who have been referred from primary care. Patients attend in the hope that their symptoms can be cured or ameliorated so that they can continue with an acceptable quality of life. Implicit in this exercise is the expertise of the hospital consultant.

In many respects referral from primary to secondary care has an inhibitory effect on the patient's input into the clinical management equation. Clearly patient input depends upon:

- patients' perception of their own health

- their expectation(s) of the consultation

- their understanding of the disease process for which they have been referred.

Most patients, faced with a new clinician in the context of the hospital specialist service, will be less in control unless they are particularly articulate with regard to their own needs and wishes. The drive within the hospital service is largely about fact finding, formulation of a diagnosis, its proof and management. The need to maximize throughput to make the most of the resources available may run counter to the needs of individual patients, who in many cases will need to have their predicament and concerns dealt with at more length.

Ideally, the consultation should function as the vehicle whereby clinician and patient can reach a joint view of the patient's state of health at that point in time, even if a clear-cut diagnostic label cannot always be applied to the patient.

Patients will reattend outpatients, and the consultations occurring within one or two visits of the first consultation may be of varying value. These early reconsultation visits may be to appraise the patient of investigations, to revise the diagnosis, possibly a prognostic formulation, and to evaluate the value of any intentions that have been made. Thereafter, unless the disorder is particularly complex, the patient will, or should, be returned to the primary care sector for further care. However, this may or may not happen, and there is evidence that in many areas too many appointments in hospital clinics are made for patients who could be cared for in primary care.

Decision making

One of the fundamental concepts that underpins the authors' flow process model is that patients' health as related to a given problem can be perceived to be in one of two alternative states, i.e. satisfactory or unsatisfactory. If either the doctor or patient feels (either subjectively or based upon objective evidence) that the state of health is not satisfactory then it must be, by definition, unsatisfactory. Restated, both clinician and patient have actively to agree that the patient's state of health is satisfactory for it to be so described. It is important to make some underlying assumptions explicit:

1   it is the clinician and patient who jointly make the assessment of the state of the patient's health

2   in order to do this standards, be they subjective or objective, implicit or explicit, must be referred to by both.

There is a body of literature relating to clinicians' decision making, of which the following summaries are particularly relevant.

Elstein *et al.*[5] devised the hypothetico-deductive theory of clinical decision making. According to this theory, the physician generates a number of hypotheses either simultaneously or rapidly in sequence very early in the clinical encounter. Between three and six hypotheses are held initially, some of which may have been generated based upon the doctor's previous knowledge of the patient. Following this the physician collects information using 'search and scan strategies' and 'cue interpretation', constantly redefining and refining the hypotheses, discarding those that do not fit with the clinical information that becomes available.

Groen and Patel[6] have cast doubt on the hypothetico-deductive theory of clinical decision making. It may be that experts as opposed to novices use 'strong' problem-solving methods that depend upon complex knowledge bases held by individual doctors. This implies that an element of pattern recognition may be more important than previously thought.

All of the above may be brought into play when decisions are made, in conjunction with the patient, as to the state of the patient's health.

This approach needs to be considered carefully, as making a precise decision on the satisfactory or unsatisfactory state of the patient's health may involve the use of extra resources that may not be available to the physician in primary care.

In the shared care process for a given disorder, agreement must be reached regarding when patients should be referred so that a definitive decision about health status can be made. A good example is the patient who presents with an itchy rash, which after initial diagnosis and treatment, is felt to be occupational eczema. The management of this patient with an unsatisfactory health status will need to be carried out in hospital as a series of investigations may be required, including:

- full occupational history
- comprehensive patch testing.

This can be seen as a series of graded steps based on standards set by accepted national practice and agreed between the primary and secondary physicians with regard to patients in their care.

Health status

Unsatisfactory health status

This category is open to considerable interpretation and input from primary and secondary care physicians, as well as from patients. It is possible for a patient to feel ill and for the general practitioner to be unable to find a cause but for the health status of the patient to be labelled as 'unsatisfactory'. It is also possible for a patient to feel well, for the consultant to record a blood pressure of 220/130 and for the health status of the patient to be recorded as 'unsatisfactory', despite the patient having no physical complaints and leading a high-quality existence with no limitations at all. In practice, the margins between satisfactory and unsatisfactory are less clearly defined than in this example, yet clearly these categories of health status should remain mutually exclusive.

The role of the secondary care physician in regard to the patient with an unsatisfactory health status can include:

- providing options and advice
- commencement of some therapeutic agent
- advice regarding surgical correction of a problem
- admission for further investigations.

There are probably few situations in which a watching brief needs to be held by a hospital physician for a patient with an unsatisfactory health status. For the hospital physician it is tempting to commission more and more investigations. It is very clear that there is continuing growth in the use of highly sophisticated investigations in hospital, which are likely to prove an important target for cost-effectiveness as an element of providing clinically efficient service.

Satisfactory health status

There are different ways for the patient to join and follow the satisfactory route within the model:

1   the patient may feel well and the clinician be satisfied with the history and examination. They will then jointly agree that the patient's health status is satisfactory. This represents an acceptable consensus. This will equally apply if the patient fails to report symptoms or the clinician fails to examine or investigate appropriately

2   the patient may wish to tolerate certain symptoms rather than have further investigations or treatment. The clinician may be prepared to accept a blood pressure of 170/100 as 'normal or acceptable' for a given patient who is tolerating the current medication and side-effects that had been very troublesome in the past with previous treatment. In this instance the clinician is prepared to alter the standards by which 'satisfactory' or 'unsatisfactory' is judged. This means that there must be some degree of compromise in regard of the different perceptions that patient and clinician may have of the clinical situation.

It is important to distinguish at this point between the severity and stability of the health status of patients. Both parties may wish to use a variety of measures for making the judgement as to 'satisfactory' or 'unsatisfactory', for example:

- subjective – can the patient work or play sport as a criterion?
- objective – peak flow rate versus normogram for an asthmatic.

A patient who suffers from a chronic illness, such as chronic obstructive airways disease, who is short of breath on gentle exercise, e.g. walking about the house, has a peak flow rate of 40% of predicted and needs to have continuous oxygen therapy obviously has severe disease that may vary in stability.

Stability

If a patient's condition is unchanging from one review to the next and both patient and clinician accept that the disease has been optimally treated, then the condition may be considered to be stable. Such a patient may be considered to be in a 'satisfactory' state regardless of the severity of symptoms. For example, a patient with asthma may be perfectly satisfied when respiratory function is stable at a peak expiratory flow rate (PEFR) of 55% of predicted. The operative factor, in terms of management, is stability. Severe chronic disease which is stable or at maximum therapy, is seen in many clinical areas. Patients, who have usually lived with the condition for many years, are well placed to judge when additional intervention is required. Subjective assessment, e.g. of epilepsy or congestive cardiac failure may be added to by simple objective measures – for instance, drug or electrolyte levels. The consequence for such patients of repeated assessment of health status as satisfactory should lead to transfer of care from the secondary to the primary sector.

Role of the patient

During the assessment of a patient there must be a two-way flow of information between patient and clinician. Patients should have a say in the aggressiveness with which the diagnosis is pursued, and in the depth of assessment.

Curiosity, especially of the secondary care physician, may lead to invasive investigations. It is essential that the benefits and drawbacks associated with a pattern of investigation, as compared with the potential disadvantages of no investigations at all, are explained to the patient, who can then have the final say in how far investigations are taken. This may mean that judgements have to be made on less than ideal information.

A triangular approach involving patient, general practitioner and consultant may lead to the best balance being struck in the interests of the patient. At the heart of any shared care system is the agreement of all parties as to what is the appropriate course of action in any given situation.

The patient may wish to accept certain symptoms to avoid a pattern of treatment if they are concerned, rightly or wrongly, about its adverse consequences. Using asthma as an example, there is ample evidence that patients, both adults and children, will tolerate quite high levels of limitation on activity rather than accept the perceived risk of the use of inhaled corticosteroids, which at low doses have not been associated with clinical complications over a 25-year period. The concerns of patients and parents need to be taken into account when determining health status. It would be hard, however, for a clinician to assign a satisfactory status to a 20-year-old asthmatic patient who:

- has PEFR of 80% in the middle of the day
- a PEFR dipping to 40% in the morning
- wakes every night coughing.

Thus whilst the patient's perception of treatment will be influenced by potential side-effects which they feel may be:

- unpleasant

- potentially harmful

the clinician should be far more swayed by the concept of 'Number Needed to Treat'. These data give the total number of patients who required treatment to prevent an episode of:

- stroke – warfarin/aspirin

- myocardial infarction – lipid lowering drugs

- gastric cancer – endoscopy in the over-45s.

Refinement of such data in the future will give a much clearer picture of the cost–benefit ratio, with side-effects being included as part of the cost side of the equation.

Watching

Patients who are in this sector of the model should be either clinically stable or pursuing interventions aimed at maintaining clinical stability following ascertainment of diagnosis. Review of the patient can be triggered in one of two ways, which will lead to another clinical assessment.

Time

It has been traditional to review patients after a set period of time. In secondary care this is the basis of a high proportion of outpatient appointments. This is done to check symptoms and signs against the agreed standards (be they implicit or explicit). If the patient's state of health remains satisfactory, especially after a number of clinical assessments, then a number of options are open to the patient and physician. If there is stability of symptoms over a series of visits such that both the patient and objective clinical measures support a satisfactory health status, then it may be possible to reduce (step down) the patient's drug treatment, to stop it altogether, or to decrease the frequency of review.

This argument applies to those patients with severe and untreatable disease who remain clinically stable, especially when both primary and secondary care clinicians agree that there is nothing further that can be done to enhance quality of life or reduce symptoms. An example is the patient with chronic obstructive pulmonary disease who has irreversible airflow limitation demonstrated by full investigation including nebulized bronchodilator therapy and a corticosteroid trial. Progression in this individual's airway disease will depend upon various factors, but it is unlikely to be influenced by repeated secondary care reviews. At a later stage when long-term oxygen therapy needs to be considered, the patient's care can be transferred from the primary to secondary sector for reassessment. In the intervening period the patient can be appropriately cared for by the general practitioner, ideally to agreed standards, for acute exacerbations of respiratory symptoms.

Observation (self-assessment by the patient)

This can be by either symptom or objective measurement. The patient may be instructed to return for a clinical assessment immediately it is felt that the clinical state becomes unsatisfactory, or given a self-management plan. In this case the patient is undertaking the process of determining health status. The clinician's input is to determine the self-assessment standards against which observations should be compared.

Self-management plan

Self-management plans require coordination between primary and second-ary care sectors and a willingness of the patient to take on an active role as observer. Areas of clinical medicine in which self-management plans have been used extensively are in the management of asthma[7] and diabetes. Such chronic conditions lend themselves to high levels of home monitoring of both subjective and objective measures. The health professional support for such a system may be either medical or nursing.

Many advantages can be postulated for giving patients control over their own illness:

1   patients are unique and should be treated as individuals

2   dosage schedules, derived from studies on groups of patients, are of nec-essity a compromise for each patient. The dynamic nature of diabetes, asthma or hypertension means that constant fine adjustments to dosage schedules may be required to achieve 'best possible control'

3   self-management of an illness encourages a responsible adult attitude towards all aspects of disease management and control

4   self-management plans encourage a 'patient-centred' approach

5   self-monitoring, e.g. of blood sugar allows immediate and sensitive adjustment of dosage. This also prevents delay whilst 'permission' is sought from medical carers to alter the medication regimen

6   accurate self-management should allow the reduction or abolition of symptoms and effects of the illness. Outcome measures such as work or

school absenteeism can be kept to a minimum whilst also allowing the minimum effective dose of medication to be used.

Point 6 above can be used to assess the effectiveness of self-management plans. Such plans, as mentioned in both national and international guidelines on the care of asthma, are a partnership between the health professional and patient. Partridge[8] made the following points about self-management plans.

- All guidelines mention the value of partnership between health professional and patient/parent, together with the adoption of written self-management plans.

- All patients with asthma deserve both oral and written advice about signs that their asthma may be worsening, e.g. wakening at night or increased use of bronchodilators. Other patients may require written advice about specific short-term changes – this greatly increases compliance. The national audit of asthma in Britain in 1991–2 showed that only 29% of patients had their own meter. Of those who had experienced an attack in the year preceding the study, only 41% had a self-management plan.[9]

There has been much debate as to the value of implementing self-management plans, and also whether subjective (symptom-based) or objective (peak flow) methodologies should be used. Studies provide evidence both for and against such plans.

A 1994 study[10] showed that a symptom-based asthma self-management plan using patient-held cards resulted in fewer days off work and less treatment, while increasing mean peak flow. It does seem reasonable that patients should understand the mechanisms of their asthma, know how to use peak flow meters and inhalers correctly and be able to conduct their own long-term management. To achieve this there is a need to facilitate the learning process and for patients to share in its implementation.[11] Certainly teaching patients how to cope with chronic disease has proved more successful in reducing morbidity than have programmes designed principally to improve patients' knowledge.[12]

However, Drummond et al.[13] found that after one year there were no significant differences between patients randomized between self-monitoring of peak flow and conventional monitoring. However, those given a peak flow meter recorded an increase in general practice consultations that was almost statistically significant. Among patients whose asthma was judged on entry to be more severe, those allocated to self-monitoring used more than twice as many oral steroids. Patients who already possessed a peak flow meter at the start of the study recorded higher morbidity over the course of the year than those eligible for randomization. The authors concluded that prescribing peak flow meters and giving self-management guidelines to all asthma sufferers is unlikely to improve mortality or morbidity. However, they also felt that patients whose asthma is severe may benefit from such an intervention.

The advantage of developing a self-management plan based upon response behaviour in consultation with the patient is that teaching patients how to cope with their chronic disease and how to respond to changes has more effect on reducing morbidity than simply increasing patients' knowledge. Hence, it is essential that the use of self-management plans within the context of shared care is based upon a full accord between patients and the primary and secondary care clinicians. The requirement is that patients should change their behaviour in response to changes in the severity of their disease and this should be an essential component of the knowledge that is imparted to patients in regard to their asthma.

This raises issues of the quality of health professionals' own knowledge base and their ability to transfer information to, and encourage behavioural change in, patients. In the current context of asthma management in primary care, there is a lack of standardized training for practice nurses and evidence that they are taking on roles for which they are not trained.

To ensure that the maximum benefits of self-management plans based on shared care are realized, such issues will need to be addressed and options devised to allow common high standards of care to be adopted.

Clinical intervention

Doing something

Inspection of the model will show that the clinician has to make a decision each time it becomes apparent that the patient's state of health is un-satisfactory. This decision reflects where and by whom the patient is to be looked after and may be most simply expressed as; 'Will I, or my team, continue to care for this patient or not?' If the answer is in the negative, then the patient will need to be referred to secondary care. It is interesting to note in passing that many decisions to refer are triggered by the sequelae of the main problem; the patient with benign prostatic hypertrophy may require admission because of acute retention of urine or chronic renal failure.

The intervention(s) will be considered successful if the patient's health status reverts to satisfactory, although it may take some time for this to happen. It is important to be clear as to what information will be required in order to know when a satisfactory state has been reattained. Diagnostic certainty[14] should be discussed with the patient. Does the patient have to know the exact diagnosis or will it be sufficient to know that there is no evidence of any serious illness?

The decision making described above is often implicit, with the clinician behaving in the same way as always. If the decision is that the patient remains within primary care, there are many interventions that a clinician can make, as described below.

Using time

This often occurs when the patient feels ill but the general practitioner can find no underlying cause. 'Come and see me in a few days if you are no better'. Again, the patient is being invited to undertake the process of 'satisfactory/unsatisfactory' self-assessment. The general practitioner may also indicate standards, e.g. 'I will see you if you:

- are still vomiting

- cough-up green phlegm

- get a headache etc.'

These tactics are often more appropriate in short-term illness. In longer standing disorders such as benign prostatic hypertrophy, the patient may have waited many months before coming to the clinician.

Investigating

Investigations are used to support or refute hypotheses. They can be important in both positive and negative senses. Abnormal tests, except in the stable chronically ill patient, will confirm that the patient's state of health is unsatisfactory and that, following the clinical assessment, most patients will require a further intervention. One or more normal test(s) may confirm to both general practitioner and patient that the state of health is satisfactory and that the patient can safely enter the observation arm of the model, albeit under treatment if required.

However, the costs of investigations are rising[15] and are a prime target for government attention, especially when there are variations in the way that investigations are being used. This area has been the subject of research within Europe, with a mean request rate for blood tests ranging from 5.1% in the UK to 15.5% in Switzerland.[16] The authors were not able to identify single factors that might explain the differences, but suggested that 'individual and/or cultural characteristics of the patient or the general practitioner, such as the quest for diagnostic certainty, disease-centred or patient-centred attitudes and medical decision making strategies should also be investigated in order to develop successful strategies for promoting optimal use of diagnostic technology'.

Thus, clinicians are being asked to defend the use of such tests in outcome rather than process terms. In France and Germany, doctors have been paid relatively less for diagnostic tests with the aim of reducing demand.[17]

Checking drug compliance/technique

This is ascertaining whether an existing drug intervention is effective, when taken properly, in the individual patient rather than whether the drug is effective *per se*. It is obviously important to know why a drug intervention has not been effective before attempting to introduce another.

Altering medication dosage

Patients could theoretically continue to loop around the 'unsatisfactory limb' of primary care indefinitely, with different explanations and interventions being offered for this. In actuality, some patients are referred, some unfortunately die. Although there are many patients in primary care with chronic illness, most come to terms with their illness, their doctor and themselves and are content to be observed in the 'satisfactory limb' of the model.

References

1 Stott N C H, Davis R H (1979) The exceptional potential in each primary care consultation. *J Roy Coll Gen Pract* **29**, 201–205.

2 McWhinney I R (1972) Problem solving and decision making in primary medical practice. *Proc Roy Soc Med* **65**, 35–38.

3 Smith D H, McWhinney I R (1975) Comparison of the diagnostic methods of family physicians and internists. *J Med Ed* **50**, 264–270.

4 Howie J G R (1974) Further observations on diagnosis and management of general practice respiratory illness using simulated patient consultations. *Br Med J* **2**, 540–543.

5 Elstein A S, Shulman L S, Sprafka S S (1978) *An Analysis of Clinical Reasoning.* Harvard University Press, Cambridge, MA.

6 Groen G J, Patel V M (1985) Medical problem-solving; some questionable assumptions. *J Med Ed* **19**, 95–99.

7 Beesley R, Cashly M, Holgate S T (1989) A self management plan in the treatment of adult asthma. *Thorax* **44**, 200–204.

8 Partridge M (1994) Asthma: guided self management (editorial). *Br Med J* **308**, 547–548.

9 Neville E G, Clark R C, Hoskins G *et al.* (1993) National asthma attack authority 1991–2. *Br Med J* **306**, 551–562.

10 D'Souza W, Crane J, Burgess C *et al.* (1994) Community based asthma care: trial of a 'credit card' asthma self management plan. *Eur Respir J* **7**, 1260–1265.

11 Charlton I (1990) New perspectives in asthma self management. *Practitioner* **234**, 30–32.

12 Sibbald B (1989) Patient self care in acute asthma. *Thorax* **44**, 97–101.

13 Drummond N, Abdalla M, Beattie J A G *et al.* (1994) Effectiveness of routine self monitoring of peak flow in patients with asthma. *Br Med Assoc* **308**, 564–567.

14 Kassirer J P (1989) Our stubborn quest for diagnostic certainty: a cause of excessive testing. *N Engl J Med* **320**, 1489–1491.

15 Broughton P M G (1990) Laboratory medicine in primary health care. *Br J Gen Pract* **40**, 2–3.

16 Leurquin P, Van Casteren V, De Maeseneer J (1995) Use of blood tests in general practice: a collaborative study in eight European countries. *Br J Gen Pract* **45**, 21–25.

17 Abel-Smith B, Mossialos E (1994) Cost containment and health care reform. A study of the European Union. *Occasional Paper in Health Policy No. 2.* LSE Health, London School of Economics and Political Science, London.

6

The transfer of patients between primary and secondary care sectors

The referral process

Referral rates vary between general practices by three- to fourfold.[1,2] Wide variations[3] have been identified in hospitalization rates for common surgical procedures and medical admissions in many Western developed countries. This is confirmed by Wilkin *et al.*,[4] who have given an account of the activities of modern general practice within the UK (Table 6.1).

In the third national morbidity study, a general practitioner with 2000 patients was found, on average, to make 240 referrals per year.[5] This is low in comparison with other countries – a testament to the effectiveness of the gatekeeper role of the general practitioner within the NHS.

Andersen and Mooney[6] believe that variation in referral rates is due to the way that clinical decisions are made. A confounding factor when considering referral rates alone is that a doctor with particular skills in one clinical area in any given practice may attract patients, or partners may internally refer.[7] This may distort that general practitioner's referral rate in that area, by increasing the number of patients that the individual general practitioner should refer. Roland[8] feels that conformity to a numeric norm is therefore an insufficient basis for deciding the appropriateness of referrals. However, it is evident that it is not clear

Table 6.1   Variation between UK general practitioners

Rates per patient	Minimum	Maximum
Consulting	<2	>5
Prescribing/100 consultations	<50	>90
Investigation/100 consultations	<1	>15
Referral/100 consultations	<3	>17

what is a desirable referral rate.[9] The conundrum that is yet to be resolved is:

- do high-referring general practitioners refer more patients unnecessarily
  than those general practitioners with low rates or

- do low-referring doctors fail to refer patients who could benefit from
  specialist treatment?

Patients have their own legitimate view on the referral process. Dowie[10]
identified four situations in which patients could initiate their own referral:

1   the patient knows that referral will be necessary because of the nature
     or complexity of the complaint

2   the patient wants a prophylactic intervention, e.g. sterilization

3   the general practitioner has failed to manage the condition and
     welcomes the patient's suggestion of referral

4   the patient demands a referral although there are no clinical grounds in
     the opinion of the GP.

There is a growing body of evidence that patient pressure can have an
influence upon referral rates. Armstrong et al.[11] reported that general
practitioners with the highest referral rates were more likely to report
pressure from patients for referral. Throughout Europe,[12] in respect of
referrals, 20% of patients are reported to have exerted a large influence,
25% a small influence and 55% nil. In The Netherlands patients exert
more influence; in Italy less. These figures tell us more about social
interaction between doctor and patient than about health care systems. In
this instance there was no difference in influence between high- or low-
referring doctors. In a recent study in the UK it was found that patients who
expect a referral are six times more likely to be referred than those who
do not.[13]

Despite this, there is also evidence that patients increasingly wish to use
secondary care services. Nearly 20% of patients surveyed in one study[14] said
that they had wanted a second opinion in the preceding two years, but only
one-third of these patients had actually asked for one. A general practitioner[15] found that, despite making practice facilities fully available, use
of casualty by patients in the practice was the equivalent of 70 surgeries
per year.

Within the clinical process model the decision to refer can be seen as a
decision to share accountability for the care of the patient. The question
that has to be asked by the clinician before referring a patient is: 'Am I
prepared to provide sole care for this patient?' If the answer is 'no', then
referral is required.

Handover of care

This is easier to define than transfer of care. In this situation the general practitioner has no immediate responsibility for the care of the patient. This occurs, for instance, in situations where a general anaesthetic is being administered. In practical terms it also happens whenever a patient is within the confines of a hospital. If the hospital deals with acute medicine then a patient who suffers a heart attack, for example, will be dealt with without reference to the general practitioner. In practical terms these situations are implicitly recognized as being outside the scope of primary care general medical services. Therefore, the general practitioner either is not informed that care has been handed over or makes the decision not to be involved, i.e. to suspend accountability with the patient. This is the situation that prevails when a patient is admitted to a hospital as an emergency by the general practitioner.

Transfer of care

This is less easy to deal with unless the situation has been fully discussed beforehand. What is the range of responsibilities and services that is to be provided by each doctor? Many complex technical procedures and investigations can only be provided by consultants. Other activities, such as taking a history, examination, interpretation of test results or confirming that a patient is fit to return to normal duties, can be provided by both consultant and general practitioner. Formalizing a clinical scope may mean that clinicians do not perform certain tasks even though they are capable of doing so.

Clinical scope[16] is defined as the protocol to be provided by a party, as determined by an accountability. For individuals clinical scope(s) forms part of the job description. An accountability can detail a number of clinical scopes.

Further consideration of this area will demonstrate that it is both possible and eminently sensible for an accountability to be set up between general practitioner and consultant before patients become involved and shared care starts. Such an accountability should form the basis of an agreement for the commencement of shared care and for the shared care parameters – to be used when the general practitioner is deciding which patients to refer and at what stage in their illness. Information can also be given indicating whether handover or transfer of care is desired. Telephone contact between clinicians can also clarify such issues. BONELINE[17] is described as a direct access service for general practitioners to orthopaedic consultants in Doncaster. It is much appreciated by general practitioners, and it was found that talking to the consultant avoided referral in nearly 25% of cases. However, there were, on average, only 2.5 calls per week to the consultants.

For most clinical problems referral from primary care to secondary care can be either acute or non-acute. In the former setting the expectations of the patient, the general practitioner and the secondary care physician may be fairly explicit and are likely to be well understood by each of the other parties. For example, in cases of acute on chronic bronchitis, urinary retention or gastrointestinal bleeding, there is a paramount need to confront the life-threatening and discomforting symptoms of the patient. The decision to refer is partly made by the patient conveying to the general practitioner the severity of the symptoms and partly the result of a recognition by the general practitioner that the patient cannot be cared for effectively in the primary care sector. Hence, the referral is made with relatively unambiguous demands on the specialist provider of care.

However, this is a picture that is probably oversimplified, and other factors may play a role in the decision on the part of the primary care clinician to refer a given patient, for example social factors in the case of patients who cannot be looked after at home because they live alone, are frail or elderly. Additionally, there may yet be limiting factors on the part of the general practitioner because of the need for high-technology diagnostic or management facilities. In the context of asthma, one study showed very clearly that many patients with acute severe asthma who are referred as an emergency to hospital could be quite safely and effectively cared for in the primary care setting if the general practitioner had the skills and the desire to care for such patients. It was found that referral rates by general practitioners who were prepared to give intravenous hydrocortisone, a high dose of oral prednisolone and nebulized β_2-agonists (normally considered baseline treatment in the hospital setting) were clearly reduced compared with referral rates by those who were only prepared to give β_2-agonists. Hence, it is possible that in the case of many disorders the demarcation between primary and secondary care is more blurred than previously supposed and that certain skills are common to practitioners on both sides of the traditional borderline between these sectors. The use of guidelines, such as those produced by the British Thoracic Society for the treatment of asthma, helps clinicians in primary and secondary care to reach agreement as to what those common skills are, and to what extent each party should be accountable for the provision of the given standard of care for an individual patient. Recognition of common skills and their appropriate delivery as close to the patient's home as possible brings an element of clinical efficiency to the desired effectiveness in medical care and, furthermore, tends to reduce variations in medical practice.

To pursue this further, clinicians in primary and secondary care need to decide what constitutes an appropriate acute referral. This should define who is referred and how, under what circumstances transfer of care should occur and what is required from secondary care by the patient and the general practitioner.

In the case of non-acute referral from primary to secondary care the objectives of the patient and general practitioner are often less clear-cut. Some patients will exert pressure on their primary care physician for referral to secondary care solely because they want a second opinion. Others will feel that their condition is such that they are no longer happy with the level of management that a general practitioner can provide. However, it is common for secondary care clinicians to see patients arising from a single specialty referral but who have multiple problems. Therefore, the consultant in the secondary care sector may be faced with performing many other roles with regard to care of these problems. This is perhaps less likely to occur in a surgical clinic, where reasons for non-acute referral are more clearly defined, e.g. breast lump, central abdominal pain, haemorrhoids or painful hip, than in a medical clinic, where a typical patient might have dyspnoea in the setting of a lifetime's cigarette consumption, hypertension, gastro-oesophageal reflux and central chest pain on exertion. In the last case the general practitioner should make some attempt to prioritize requirements from secondary care; otherwise there is a danger that the generalist consultant in secondary care will take on all of the problems and become effectively the primary care physician for that patient. This has long been a criticism of hospital practice; however, as the reduction in provision of secondary care progresses, it will no longer be possible for hospital physicians to maintain this role.

The discharge process

The transfer of care from secondary to primary sectors is a reversal of the referral process. The transfer of a patient into primary care may follow an acute hospital admission or be the return to primary care of a patient who has been the subject of secondary care consultation and investigation. These two types of discharge require the transfer of different information.

Following the discharge of a patient with a recent acute medical problem, such as asthma, pneumonia or gastrointestinal bleeding, to primary care, information may be communicated by a doctor's letter, usually written by a junior member of the secondary care team, which leaves the hospital on the same day that the patient is discharged, either with the patient or via normal postal services. The second line of information is the full hospital summary of the patient's admission. This may arrive at a variable period of time after discharge and may be written by almost any grade of doctor in the secondary care team. There is great variation in the content of information in both of these documents, and Table 6.2 gives an outline of the information that may be needed when a patient is discharged from hospital after an episode of acute severe asthma. An audit of this information of transfer suggests that requirements are poorly complied with. Development of quality standards, enforceable through the contracting process, may address some of the issues. In particular, the time between a patient's

Table 6.2 Information to be transferred from secondary to primary care when a patient with asthma is discharged from hospital

- severity of asthma at admission
- peak expiratory flow rate (PEF) on admission
- predicted or best known PEF
- PEF at discharge
- inhaler technique and device checked
- medication at discharge to include dose, frequency and duration
- educational update given
- management plan discussed with patient
- outpatient appointment arranged and date included

discharge from hospital and the arrival of the full discharge summary at the GP practice is an important focus for setting appropriate standards of information, together with the speed of transfer of that information.

The transfer of information relating to hospital outpatient visits and the final transfer of the patient back to primary care is likely to be in the form of a letter and, unlike the hospital discharge summary, is more likely to be written by the consultant or a senior member of the junior medical team. Again, the information provided in such letters may vary greatly and be of limited usefulness to both the patient and the primary care physician. A suggested outline of the minimum content (datasets) for the letter to the general practitioner after a patient consultation is given in Table 6.3.

Nurse-to-nurse discharge

With the growing number of nurse specialists in secondary care, the prospect of nurse-to-nurse discharge from secondary to primary care becomes a reality. This is possible if nurses are working to common protocols that provide for the transfer of stable patients on a semi-automatic basis, e.g. three consecutive assessments of a satisfactory health status. In the context of the care of patients with chronic persistent asthma, the role of the nurse practitioner in both primary and secondary care has increased in the last decade, and this would be an appropriate area for direct nurse-to-nurse transfer. Providing similar levels of training with regard to asthma care for nurses would allow them to communicate more effectively, perhaps more than their medical colleagues do. This approach to the handling of a high proportion of patients with asthma in a variety of centres appears to find favour with both health professionals and patients alike.

Ante-natal care is an example of how such concepts can be taken further when combined with modern technology. The Welsh Domiciliary Foetal Monitoring project used the public telephone system to transmit, via a

Table 6.3   Minimum data set of information to be included in letter to general practitioner from outpatient consultation

• Diagnosis	– COPD
	– other diagnoses
• Current status	
• Main daytime symptom	• Main nocturnal symptom
– none	– none
– cough	– cough
– wheeze	– wheeze
– tightness	– tightness
– shortness of breath	– shortness of breath
• Sputum	– daily
	– purulent
	– mucopurulent
	– mucoid
• Restriction of activity – level	– walking on flat
	– climbing stairs
	– household duties
	– shopping
	– work
	– hobbies
	– sport
	– none
• Peak expiratory flow rate	(a) actual
	(b) predicted
• Current medication	
• Recommendations	– discharge or date of follow-up
• Item to be selected	

modem, foetal heart monitoring traces in 'high risk' pregnancies. Project results[18,19] suggest:

• reduction of time spent in hospital amongst this population of high risk mothers

• lower anxiety levels in high risk women monitored at home

• maternal satisfaction with the service provided.

Location of care can be shifted, in this instance, to the patient's home with all the attendant advantages of reduction in travel, whilst allowing care to be provided to an acceptable standard. As is argued in the next chapter such considerations are central to the planning of future health care delivery.

References

1 Wilkin D, Smith A (1989) Variations in general practitioners' referral rates to consultants. *J Roy Coll Gen Pract* **37**, 350–353.

2 Noone A, Goldacre M, Coulter A *et al.* (1989) Do referral rates vary widely between practices and does supply of services affect demand? *J Roy Coll Gen Pract* **39**, 404–407.

3 Sanders D, Couter A, McPherson K (1989) *Variation in Hospital Admission Rates: a Review of the Literature.* King's Fund, London.

4 Wilkin D (1987) *Anatomy of Urban General Practice.* Tavistock, London.

5 Royal College of General Practitioners, Office of Population Censuses and Surveys, DHSS (1986) *1981–1982 Morbidity Statistics from General Practice: Third National Study.* HMSO, London.

6 Andersen T F, Mooney G (1990) *The Challenges of Medical Practice Variations.* Macmillan Press, London.

7 Reynolds D, Chitnis J G, Roland M (1991) General practitioner referrals: do good doctors refer more patients to hospital? *Br Med J* **301**, 98–102.

8 Roland M (1992) Measuring appropriateness of hospital referrals. In *Hospital Referrals* (eds M Roland, A Coulter), p. 141. Oxford University Press, Oxford.

9 Wilkin D, Metcalfe D H, Marinker M (1989) The meaning of information of GP referrals to hospitals. *Community Medicine* **11**(1), 65–70.

10 Dowie R (1983) *General Practitioners and Consultants: a Study of Outpatient Referrals.* King Edward's Hospital Fund for London, London.

11 Armstrong D, Fry J, Armstrong P (1991) Doctors' perceptions of pressure from patients for referral. *Br Med J* **302**, 1186–1188.

12 COMAC-HSR in collaboration with European General Practice Research Workshop (1992) The European study of referrals from primary to secondary care. *Occasional Paper No. 56.* Royal College of General Practitioners, London.

13 Webb S, Lloyd M (1994) Prescribing and referral in general practice: a study of patients' expectations and doctors' actions. *Br J Gen Pract* **44**, 165–169.

14 College of Health (1991) *Which Way to Health?* February, 32–35.

15 Singh S (1988) Self referral to accident and emergency department: patients' perceptions. *Br Med J* **297**, 1179–1180.

16 NHS Management Executive (1992) *The Clinical View of the Common Basic Specification. The Cosmos Project Clinical Process Model Version 2.0.* NHS Management Executive, Birmingham.

17 Roland M O, Bewley B (1992) BONELINE: evaluation of an initiative to improve telephone communication between general practitioners and specialists. *J Publ Health Med* **14**(3), 307–309.

18 Dawson A J, Middlemiss C, Jones E M *et al.* (1988) Fetal heart monitoring by telephone 1: Development of an integrated system in Cardiff. *Br J Obstet Gynaecol* **95**, 1018–1023.

19 Middlemiss C, Dawson A J, Gough N *et al.* (1989) A randomized study of a domiciliary antenatal care scheme: maternal psychological effects. *Midwifery* **5**, 69–74.

7

Implementing shared care schemes

A vision for the future of shared care

In the authors' view, the patient will be the focus around which care will be both organized and managed in the future. Our model has much in common with flow process modelling,[1] which is more commonly found, at the present time, in industrial settings. It provides a framework for examining the service from the patient's (consumer's) point of view. The stages in patients' use of a service can be broken down into steps. The problems that a patient may encounter at each step can also be identified, studied and resolved. It is this emphasis on the patient's perspective that makes the methodology of flow process audit particularly valuable. At the present time there may well be misunderstanding among patient, general practitioner and consultant as to the purpose of referral. The patient's wish for explanation and reassurance is often not seen as a legitimate reason for referral by consultants and may not be communicated to them by general practitioners.[2] Patients often have a different perspective from either general practitioner or consultant on the referral process. In one study only in 33% of referrals did all three parties agree as to the purpose of referral.[3] A study of patients referred to hospital found that patients often have a realistic view of the probable effectiveness of treatment, but would like to have more information about the nature of their problem and its prognosis than is often provided.[4]

Dowie[5] has suggested that a substantial part of the reason for the variability in family doctors' referral rates lies in their cognitive processes – differing confidence in their clinical judgement and differing awareness of the base rate probabilities of the occurrence of life threatening events. Jones[6] feels that general practitioners vary widely in the amount of information that they require to solve problems. It is suggested that clinicians possess unique and complex knowledge bases. Individual clinicians are at the centre of the reasoning process, and the intellectual and emotional context in which decisions are made will be different for each of them. The net result of this is that each GP has a unique referral threshold.[7] This is dependent on many factors:

- the personality of the GP
- the GP's willingness to take risks
- the GP's perceptions of the availability of services.

The emphasis in future shared care schemes will, therefore, be on the management of patients (taking full account of their views) with the use of appropriate skills, rather than on the location of care. This will only be possible after the clinicians, in both the primary and secondary sectors, who are involved in the care of a group of patients have decided the 'rules' that they wish to apply to the joint care of the patients, and how these will be translated into decision making. Three ways of exerting influence on doctor's decision making have been identified.[8]

1   standards – these are meant to be applied rigidly; violation constitutes poor practice

2   guidelines – they are flexible and, although they should be usually followed, they must be tailored to individual needs. In order to be able to compile a guideline, at least a number of the outcomes of a given intervention must be known

3   options – these apply when information is incomplete or the evidence indicates several equally effective courses of action.

It is likely in most scenarios that guidelines[9] will be adopted with the aim of:

- improving clinical management
- facilitating more cost-effective use of limited resources.

The NHS system, which has historically been based on generalists acting as gatekeepers to secondary care, is a cost-effective model that has been emulated by several health maintenance organizations in the United States in an attempt to contain costs.[10] The NHS reforms since 1990 have meant the start of a process of shifting resources to primary care, with general practitioners adopting a commissioning role with the aim of providing more care in the community.

One response has been the setting up of outreach clinics.[11] The current accepted wisdom is that the general practitioner accepts the responsibility for making an initial decision on every problem presented by patients

and that 90% of problems are dealt with within the practice. An awareness of:

- psychological factors

- social factors

- history taking

- examination

informs the synthesis of both a diagnosis and management plan. Part of the
plan is to help patients interpret and cope with illness[12] and to refer when
appropriate.

There is a danger that outreach clinics may eventually provide open
access for patients without referral. Such routine open access to specialist
clinics would increase the likelihood of overinvestigation of patients with
psychosomatic illness and encourage the operation of Balint's 'collusion
of anonymity',[13] whereby no clinician takes overall responsibility for the
patient. The current referral system enables the patient to have two opinions:
that of the specialist about a specific disease and that of the GP who knows
the family and patient and the context of the problem. Self-referrals to
specialists often generate follow-up appointments to review progress – these
are more appropriately the responsibility of the general practitioner. Specialists often tend to refer to other specialists when they encounter problems
outside their sphere of competence, many of which could be managed by
the general practitioner.

'The erosion of the referral system would be likely to slow the development of specialist medicine and make it less effective, efficient and innovative.'[14] How can shared care be implemented without eroding the referral
system and increasing the danger that outreach clinics will lead to open
access secondary care?

A multidisciplinary approach

Discussion about shared care usually focuses upon the interface between
primary and secondary care. It should not be forgotten that within these
domains there are multidisciplinary teams that derive a common aim and
purpose in terms of treating the patients that they care for.

In Wales, there has been much emphasis on applying technology purpose-
fully rather than just for its own sake. The principles of *Strategic Intent and
Direction for the NHS in Wales,* published in December 1989,[15] are that:

1   investment must be led by organizational development and training in
     the use and support of information systems

2   information systems must be justified by the benefits they bring to patients from improved clinical and managerial decision making

3   information for management and direction should be derived from operational systems

4   the integration of systems is essential to reduce costs and improve accuracy

5   key users of information must be involved in, and committed to, the use of information and the development of new systems

6   responsibility for data quality should be as close to the operational level as is practicable

7   data confidentiality and responsibility for data must be respected.

The ability to provide, use and manage information as a key resource is seen to be absolutely essential. The information and information technology strategy signalled NHS Wales' clear recognition of the fundamental role that information has to play in enabling organizations to make better decisions and achieve better patient care. The strategy sets out the supporting actions required to enable patient care, including its quality, to be better planned and managed within available resources. These actions include organizational development, improvements in medical records, use of diagnosis-related groups and costing of, support for and information on the management of resources.

How can these concepts be applied to the way in which data are collected by all members of the team to ensure that useful information is provided for all team members? Much of the information that is collected by attached primary health care staff is stored on records other than the patient's GP-held medical record. This means that, until electronic medical records can be fully distributed, sharing records between sites will result in incomplete transfer of information. In the short-term it would seem sensible for there to be one primary care record that could be used and accessed by all those working within a general practice.

Confidentiality of the medical record, whether computerized or not, is a matter of great concern. The issues surrounding confidentiality are complex and will not be discussed in detail in this book. Those who wish to study the issue more deeply are referred to the work by Darley et al.[16]

The attachment of social workers to practices has brought these issues even more to the fore. Non-medical staff have always had a duty to preserve confidentiality, as laid down by Korner[17] in 1984.

In the course of your duties you may have access to confidential material about patients, members of staff or other health service business. On no account must information relating to identifiable patients be divulged to anyone other than authorized persons for example medical, nursing or professional staff as appropriate who are concerned directly with the care, diagnosis or treatment of the patient. If you are in any doubt whatsoever as to the authority of a person or body asking for information of this nature you must seek advice from a superior officer. Similarly, no information of a personal or confidential nature concerning individual members of staff should be divulged to anyone without the proper authority having first been given. Failure to observe these rules will be regarded by your employer as serious and will result in disciplinary action being taken against you, including dismissal.

In respect of social services staff, the Department of Health[18] stated in 1988 that, 'if further disclosure is proposed for a purpose associated with the provision of health care, then the appropriate health professional must be consulted and his consent obtained'. This accords with the code of ethics of the British Association of Social Workers[19] whose 11th principle states that members should always ensure 'confidentiality of information and divulgence only by consent or exceptionally in evidence of serious danger'.

In summary, personal health information given to social services staff by a health professional can only be disclosed:[16]

1 in compliance with a court order

2 in compliance with a statutory requirement

3 so that health care can be provided to a client or patient for the purposes of care.

The way forward – 'internal' shared care

It is necessary here to return to Donabedian's[20] three criteria by which the quality of medical care can be evaluated:

1 structure – the resources available to the doctor

2 process – what the doctor does to or for the patient

3 outcome – the resulting changes in the health of the patient

and to adapt them to the modern multidisciplinary team. The structure of the medical record also needs to be considered. It forms the basis of the resource that is common to all team members for the exchange of information. Medical records in the 1990s tend to be organized via a summary system whether they are recorded via computer or paper system.

Computer-based summaries tend to be organized in terms of diagnoses, with all those events that can be labelled with a 'Read' code being grouped together. The structure is akin to a relational database. Examination of a patient's record will reveal the frequency with which a given code is recorded. This is very useful for gathering 'top-down' morbidity data, but is very limited in describing a patient's 'health career' or any outcome measures.

The usual measures of process held within the data record are:

- prescribing

- investigation

- referral

which again are 'Read' coded. The next step in collating team activity will be to allow all team members the opportunity to record their activity as it relates to any given diagnosis. This does not mean that keyboard skills must be learnt immediately. A method of data collection via paper records that can be transcribed 'in-house' will be perfectly adequate.

Table 7.1   Team member activity

Diagnosis	Team member	Activity
Diabetes	Doctor	Prescribing
	Practice nurse	Lifestyle advice; HbA$_1$C
	District nurse	Anti-smoking clinic
Post-operative wound infection	Doctor	Prescribing
	Practice nurse	Wound management
	District nurse	Wound management
Childhood immunizations	Health visitor	Health education
	Doctor	First DPPT and Hib
	Practice nurse	Second and third DPPT and Hib

Audit of this information would allow a matrix to be constructed which could describe the activity of each team member (Table 7.1). The next stage would involve the setting of outcome targets (Table 7.2) for individual or

Table 7.2   Outcome measures for team member activity

Diagnosis	Inputs	Outcome measures
Asthma	Doctor × 6 Practice nurse × 6 District nurse × 3	PEFR versus predicted; symptom scores; time off work; smoking status
Post-operative wound infection	Doctor × 2 District nurse × 7	Number of weeks for wound to heal; able to return to work
Childhood immunizations	Health visitor × 4 Doctor × 1 Practice nurse × 2	Immunization status

groups of patients. It would also be possible to record the site of activity (surgery/home) and for those treated at home whether the patient is:

- medically housebound, i.e. does not leave the house for any reason

- socially housebound, i.e. lacks transport to attend surgery.

While it would not be possible to calculate the input for each team member in terms of cost-effectiveness, it would certainly be possible to identify those teams that achieved their outcome measures. The methodologies that such teams used could then be disseminated as examples of 'best practice'.

Sharing information and shared access

The distributed medical record

It should be the aim of clinical information systems to supply comprehensive clinical data at any time at the 'point of service', whatever that may be. This dream has not yet been realized, but most of the information technology required to turn the dream into reality is now available.

The comprehensive clinical record is made up from data created by primary, secondary and tertiary clinicians, pathology laboratories, physiology laboratories, radiology departments, nurses, physiotherapists and pharmacies. Superimposed on top of these clinical records most hospitals run a patient administration system that holds demographic data and is used for booking clinics and hospital admissions. Although most of the information created by each of these components is currently held in paper form, computer applications are available to replace this archaic method. However, the aggregation of computerized data from each of the health service components held on disparate computer systems is rarely feasible without significant overheads in terms of computer programming, computer performance and cost.

Three principal strategies can be used to provide the comprehensive clinical health record:

1   the first solution is to hold all clinical information in one massive database to which all authorized clinicians should be given access. This is an impracticable solution for several reasons:

    - computer performance would be miserably poor

    - technical failures would paralyse all health services

    - all information needs would have to be anticipated in advance

2   the second solution allows each health care unit to develop its own clinical database and then to integrate the data by building interfaces between the disparate systems. Unfortunately, building interfaces is extremely expensive, particularly if no standard data structure is used in clinical information systems. Furthermore, interfaces frequently perform slowly as they rely on the creation of data files by one system that can be read by a second system

3   the third solution uses object-oriented technology and a shared (standard) data structure. Object-oriented databases hold information as data objects in an 'object space'. Each database has its own object space, and within the object space each object (data element) has an individual identification code. An *object request broker* (ORB) is a software tool that allows the representation of objects in a remote object space. Thus, by using an ORB, data in one clinical system can be used in a disparate clinical system so long as the data structures used in both systems are compatible. ORBs have been developed that can distribute data between databases separated by networks and running on different types of computers running different operating systems. The ORB technology is still rather immature but is currently being adopted by banks and large corporate enterprises; it is likely that this technology will form the basis of distributed clinical information systems in the future.

The computer software industry has a number of new technologies that are aimed at providing distributed information systems. The goal is to create unlimited client–server systems, where clients are applications providing functionality to the user and servers are data stores, which may reside on the same computer or any other networked computer.[21]

Systems in current use or development are based on standard query language (SQL) databases; these are relational databases (based around tables of data) linked by SQL. Many manufacturers have developed their own versions of SQL databases and related applications, but unfortunately there are no defined standards to which they all conform. Therefore client–server applications are limited by database and application compatibility.

It is widely predicted that the key technology for the future of client–server systems will be distributed objects – object-oriented databases and applications that are connected by object request brokers. Industry leaders have formed an international standards body (the Object Management Group) that has defined an architecture for distributing objects in advance of the technology being released on the commercial market.

Clearly, the electronic linking of sites so that a patient's record can be distributed and accessed from a number of locations means that:

1   the site of data entry is irrelevant

2   data only have to be entered once.

This is a more sophisticated usage of such links than has hitherto been envisaged. In Pringle's study[22] 90% of GPs were enthusiastic about electronic links with the hospital. Most frequently mentioned uses were receiving laboratory results, discharging letters, notification of admission and booking outpatient appointments directly.

What, then, if the patient were linked to the system? The patient would be able to enter data such as peak flow recordings or scores of symptoms. Because of the nature of the shared care model, a proposed link between computers to a distributed medical record, the consultant at an NHS Trust hospital would be able to interrogate the data that the nurse had already gathered or the patient supplied. This information would be instantly available to general practitioners on the circuit, and the nurse would be able to communicate immediately to all parties decisions made with regard to patients and their management.

The example that the authors explore refers specifically to asthma but should be considered as an exemplar for the generic use of this technology and the principle of shared care.

The essence of the model is that each contact with the patient gives a 'snapshot' of the patient's health at that moment. Most of the evidence that is used is collected at the time of the assessment, although patients were asked about their health in the time since they were last seen, and diary information (e.g. peak flow rates, symptom scores etc.) may also be collected.

Discussion of the 'evidence', both subjective and objective, influences the decision to be made, in primary or secondary care, as to whether the health of the patient is satisfactory or unsatisfactory, and the subsequent management. This applies however the shared care is organized and the medical record is distributed.

The diagnosis of asthma is made by demonstrating >15% variation in lung function – usually peak flow rate. This measure is therefore very important as an indicator of disease and is also simple to measure (not withstanding the variability of peak flow meters).

If the age, sex and height of the patient are held within the computer then it is possible to display graphically:

- predicted peak flow (and centiles)

- best ever recorded (and date)

- worst ever recorded (and date)

- today's reading – which adds to the sum of the data stored about the patient.

This observation will take the nurse and patient some way towards deciding whether the health of the patient is (or has been) satisfactory or unsatisfactory.

History taking or eliciting symptoms is also important. Paper record or computer screens can be designed on an algorithmic basis so that the following information can be collected.

1   Have symptoms been present?   Yes/No

If yes:

2   Which is the predominant symptom at night:

  –   shortness of breath?

  –   wheeze?

  –   tightness?

and then:

3   For how many nights per week?

4   Are activities of daily living impaired?   Yes/No

If yes:

5   Are you unable to:

  –   work?

  –   shop?

  –   do housework?

  –   walk upstairs?

  –   walk about the house?

6   How many times in the last week have you used your bronchodilator?

7   Finally record if the patient is satisfactory or unsatisfactory.

Within this scenario the decision taken by the clinician and patient of the state of the patient's health and therefore the subsequent management plan is based upon:

1   immediate objective data

2   historic subjective data

with outcome measures (satisfactory/unsatisfactory) rather than process being measured.

Peak flow rates can be recorded using electronic devices and the signal thus generated could be sent anywhere in the world. Patients could either use a simple peak flow meter and enter their data via the keyboard or enter flow into a meter directly linked into the network. Patients, especially in clinical trials, can be asked to collect both subjective and objective information via a diary card system. It is known, however, that patients may enter such data retrospectively. 'Time-stamped' data could therefore be entered into the patient's record, together with any symptom recording method.

Telemedicine

Recent advances in telecommunications enable knowledge to be disseminated far more widely than has been possible to date. To access knowledge it is no longer necessary to travel to wherever the holder of that knowledge happens to be located. Real-time audio and video equipment, transmitting signals over a telecommunications network, can enable instantaneous telepresence of the knowledge holder at a distant site. There is thus considerable potential for altering the way in which opinion from the secondary care sector is sought. The weaknesses of the traditional approach of sending the patient to be physically present with the consultant in a distant site have already been explored. The approach of deploying consultants into primary care by means of outreach clinics also has drawbacks, which will be further amplified below in the section on dermatology, a discipline in which this approach has been actively pursued for some time now.

Using telemedicine, it is possible for the consultant to remain at his hospital base but be in real-time contact with the primary care physician and patient, both located in the general practice. Linked in this fashion, a three-way consultation can take place, with input from all parties. There are numerous potential advantages to this approach and much research is ongoing.

For the patient the advantages are not having to travel to a distant site, the avoidance of the stress of visiting an alien institution and the presence of the GP or member of practice staff to act as both spokesman and advocate if necessary.

For the general practitioner it is possible to ensure that the consultant is aware of the broader picture of the patient's problems and that the consultant answers the needs of both the patient and general practitioner; a process that is not facilitated by the present outpatient-based consulting system.

For the consultant it is possible to glean far more information than is presented in a typical referral letter, to do so in a timely fashion and to ensure that advice is addressing the patient's real problems. Because there is no need to move from the base location, the considerable time wasted in travelling to and from outreach clinics can be avoided, thus releasing more time to be spent in patient contact.

For all parties there are less tangible benefits, particularly the greater interpersonal contact that such an approach offers. Many patients have expressed the view that, having discussed their health at a video consultation, they feel as though they have already met the consultant and so are much more relaxed if they should subsequently need to meet face to face.

A much closer working relationship between the consultant and general practitioner is inherent in this approach, as they are seeing and talking to each other and interacting about problems, rather than simply sending pieces of paper backwards and forwards between each other, i.e. the patient's management plan can be developed simultaneously rather than sequentially.

The goal of ending medical contact with either a satisfactory or unsatisfactory outcome can be achieved more readily with a teleconsulting service as all three parties can now be involved in deciding whether a satisfactory point has been reached. There is an opportunity for any one party who feels that this is not the case to air this view to the other two parties jointly.

During teleconsultations it is also possible to transmit data files, and thus it would be possible to transmit the specialist's own information pack with regard to a particular condition to the GP and patient during the consultation.

If teleconsulting could be combined with an electronic shared medical record then an even more exciting prospect could be in view. Not only could the consultation process be shared live, but it would also be feasible to share a document outlining the problems and outcomes encountered during that particular consultation, together with agreements about the need or otherwise for continued involvement of the secondary sector. We could thus see the breakdown of traditional barriers and facilitate the development of true patient-focused care, based in the primary care setting but sharing the expertise of the secondary sector where appropriate. This integrated approach could offer a much more efficient use of resources than is achieved using the present model.

Telemedicine offers opportunities other than simply teleconsulting. One could, for instance, enable district nurses to have direct access to wound care specialists, specialist nurse practitioners or hospital consultants to take part in interactive learning programmes or to advise on particular problems. A telemedicine project in Wales has already found it to be acceptable to all parties that nurse practitioners generate direct referrals of patients with difficult leg ulcers for a telemedicine consultation with a consultant dermatologist, a process that has been mutually beneficial.

A new dimension added to shared care by the deployment of telemedicine is that the GP and patient can choose which specialist they wish to be involved in sharing care. Because these systems are geographically independent, the GP is no longer tied to a limited choice of specialists who happen to be located in the same geographical area. If it is more appropriate to gain expertise from a distant site, then this poses no problems. This should be a major driver to ensure continuous improvement in the services offered by secondary providers, as they will not be able to rely on the inertia of the locality guaranteeing them referrals but will depend on the consultants meeting the needs of general practitioners and their patients – otherwise referrals will go elsewhere.

The sharing of care during a video consultation offers a tremendous opportunity for education of all parties involved. The traditional outpatient referral has virtually no such capacity. The development of telemedicine consulting could therefore offer an opportunity for continuous medical education. In Wales, tutors are already recognizing that time spent in video consultation should be accredited for continuing medical education (CME) purposes.

The development of telemedicine should not be driven by technology, but rather the technology should be exploited to assist in problem solving. Shared care utilizing this approach offers exciting prospects, but as with every other aspect of sharing there will be some resistance from certain parties as traditional power structures are eroded by this approach. In the long-term this can only be for the good, but those of us working in this area should plan with this factor in mind – trying to encourage colleagues to understand the benefits of such an approach and so encourage them to participate.

Telemedicine-assisted shared care offers the prospect of a radical redefinition of the role of, and interactions between, primary and secondary care. The quality of patient care should be significantly improved in a very cost-effective manner.

An example of shared care in dermatology supported by telemedicine

Undergraduate medical students receive a very limited amount of training in dermatology. Following graduation those doctors training for a career in general practice are not required to undergo any training in dermatology. Only a minority of doctors are given any significant training in dermatology, and it is then very much a hospital-oriented approach. Approximately 10% of consultations in general practice are about skin problems and almost all individuals can expect to have a significant skin problem at some point in their life.

Given the above, it is hardly surprising that many general practitioners feel that they are inadequately prepared for dealing with the plethora of skin problems that present to them. Many will try to improve their own education by attending meetings, arranging attachments to a local hospital dermatology unit or reading various journals, but few feel confident that they can deal with the majority of skin problems presenting in practice.

The prevalence of certain skin diseases such as skin cancers and atopic eczema is increasing rapidly. The secondary care sector is in danger of being swamped by the demands placed on it. If the present system of hospital-based outpatient dermatology advice is to cope, then considerable further resources will need to be devoted to this.

Outreach clinics have been suggested as a means of addressing some of the above problems, but unfortunately the average number of patients seen in such a clinic is low. In addition, some patients need to travel to hospital subsequently in any case, and the travelling time to and from the clinics by consultants means that their time is used inefficiently.

To optimize dermatology care we need to develop a system that uses the scarce specialists' skills efficiently, increases the skills of general practitioners and delivers care in a timely fashion in an appropriate setting for the patient. These factors have led to the development of teleconsulting, whereby the GP and consultant can share in the decision making and problem-solving processes by a consultation, in which the patient is physically present with the GP in the surgery and linked to the consultant at a distant site by electronic means that permit real-time video, audio and data transfer. At present, referrals for use of such a service are paper-based but a shared electronic medical record would be preferred, and this is being explored. Consulting in this fashion dramatically improves communications between GPs and consultants and automatically moves the process from one of transfer of care to shared care; shared not only between the doctors but also with the patient.

Because of the interactive nature of teleconsulting, skill transfer is inevitable and rapid. Early studies have shown that the diagnostic acumen of GPs is improving and they are also undertaking surgical procedures that previously they would automatically have referred to the secondary sector.

Time spent in contact over such a link can also be used for informal discussion about problems, as well as the development of protocols of care.

Once the principle of 'teledermatology' is accepted, it is possible to explore new areas. The high-definition images captured as part of such a service could be built into a comprehensive electronic picture library that could be an invaluable educational tool, shared by both primary and secondary care workers. Interactive CD-ROMs are being developed at present to enable CME in dermatology for general practitioners.

The roles of members of the health care team change. District nurses in Wales are already directly referring patients with difficult leg ulcers for the teleconsulting opinion of a dermatologist. Shortly they will be taking a camera with them when visiting patient's homes and will film the ulcers so that the patient will not even have to visit the general practice. The district nurse can subsequently discuss the problem with the GP, consultant, or both, using telemedicine, sharing the problem and enabling appropriate advice to be given without the patient having to leave home. Given the access to support over such a network, one could even argue that nurse specialists should be allowed to carry out minor surgical procedures on general practice premises, discussing any possible problems with the consultant directly, using the telemedicine equipment. Numerous other suggestions are being explored at the present time as interest in this area is burgeoning.

SCAMP – a pilot shared care scheme

The Shared Care Asthma Management Project (SCAMP) has arisen out of the activity that took place in the West Cardiff pilot site of the Personal Health Summary System (PHSS) project, which was a Welsh Office-sponsored project run by the Centre for Health Informatics of University College, Aberystwyth, to develop a personal health summary system. The PHSS project had the aim of altering clinical practice through the development of a novel computer system that would facilitate sharing of clinical records. The focus of the project in West Cardiff has been upon respiratory medicine and, in particular, asthma. A 'generic approach' has been adopted, which will allow the products of the project to be implemented into other clinical areas also.

The intention was to link the two establishments using ISDN technology. The software that has been developed uses object-oriented technology and C++ language and can be mapped to the clinical process model.[23]

Since the scheme began, the following actions have taken place:

1 terminals for SCAMP software have been established in two consulting rooms at Ely Bridge Surgery

2 asthma clinics have been re-established at Ely Bridge Surgery. The minimum data set collected for each patient is, at the present time, being duplicated on to the practice's AAH Meditel clinical computer system. The appropriate 'Read' codes have been created so that the information can be recorded independently of the SCAMP system

3 SCAMP terminals have been installed in Llandough Hospital. As there is not an established computerized clinical system, a paper system allowing capture of the minimum data set has been introduced for those clinicians not using SCAMP.

The next stage of the project will be the establishment of a firm base in both Llandough Hospital and Ely Bridge Surgery so that an increasing number of clinicians can begin to use SCAMP and contribute to its database. This will allow analysis of outcome measures such as:

• health status

• management plan

• location of subsequent care.

A telemedicine link will be established to cater for patients who are found to have 'unsatisfactory' health status. This work will also focus on the acceptability of such technology to those patients who use it.

Technical solutions that have been provided in the past to solve issues surrounding shared care and the medical record have failed. This has typically been because they did not address the cultural barriers involved in transcending the primary/secondary care interface. Providing attractive 'front ends' to idiosyncratic systems for shared care has been relatively easy. The task of establishing a firm base so that the care provided to patients is improved is much harder but of much greater long-term value.

Stakeholders who have already signed up to this project are those who wish to see a more cost-effective use of limited NHS resources. The ultimate outcome measure will be the impact upon the patients, who are both the consumers and funders of the service.

Priorities within a cost-limited service are always a matter of some contention. It is not intended to devote large amounts of capital to creating another new clinical system. The resources that are devoted to this project will help to improve the care for the only chronic disease within the UK, the prevalence of which is actually increasing, while demonstrating its general applicability to other aspects of clinical care.

The issues that have driven the scheme can be summarized as:

1   a perceived lack of the impact of computing on clinical care of individual patients has, in the past, led to:

   −   a top-down approach to data collection

   −   recording of diagnostic label, rather than process or outcome

   −   clinical systems that are 'data rich, information poor'.

2   the development of the Shale–Edwards model of shared care, wherein:

   −   clinical assessment should meet agreed minimum standards of care regardless of location

   −   patients' health status should be determined as 'satisfactory' or 'unsatisfactory' via a consensus method between clinicians and patients

   −   patients should clearly understand the criteria of self-observation by which they seek further medical care

   −   intervention by clinician should take place in light of patients' goals for the management of their asthma.

3   the ability to collect a computerized medical record minimum data set. In SCAMP, many items of information are being collected − partly to

assess their value in a shared care system. Our view at the present time is that the following will prove to be the core data items:

- objective respiratory function tests (PEF) expressed as a percentage of predicted normal

- asthma status of patients, as defined in the Shale–Edwards model

- a management plan decided with patients in the light of the personal goals set by patients for the outcome of their care.

SCAMP will permit, for the first time, prospective clinical interface audit to be undertaken. The object-oriented infrastructure that is being used to develop the software allows for rapid, iterative prototyping, while also ensuring that the environment will allow SCAMP to assimilate other novel technologies such as telemedicine and the electronically distributed medical record.

The electronically distributed medical record

While SCAMP is only dealing with one chronic disease in the shared care setting, the potential for health gain for the patient is much greater than in the administrative scenario that is painted by Pringle's paper.[22] If one takes yet another leap of imagination, what would happen if the patient were linked into the system? The patient would be able to enter data, such as peak flow recordings or scores of symptoms.

Patterns of variability could be recognized automatically, with alarms being triggered if PEF were to fluctuate beyond preset limits. Such alarms could trigger appointments or even admissions. The current evidence[24] is that such monitoring is most appropriate in those with severe asthma, who represent the group in which most asthma deaths occur.

The incorporation of telemedicine techniques into SCAMP is seen as an important step forward. The integration of a shared medical record, which will provide an agreed minimum set of data (much in graphic and tabular form), into a real-time three-way consultation provides many exciting possibilities, which have already been recognized in the telemedicine project, viz.:

1   achieving the aims of the consultation

2   allowing general practitioners to act as an advocate for their patients

3   sparing patients from an area of medium deprivation a two-bus journey to the hospital

4   allowing management plans to be agreed by all three involved parties; patients will know why they are attending the hospital before they arrive

5   providing two-way educational opportunities between general practice and hospital.

In order for the above to be realized, we must be certain that the consultation via computer technology meets its aims and objectives. There is a large body of literature concerning consultation within general practice. Neighbour[25] lists five checkpoints for the consultation:

1   connecting

2   summarizing

3   handing over

4   safety netting

5   housekeeping.

It must be remembered, however, that, as we propose that there are three individuals involved, the telemedicine consultation is a consultation within a consultation. It may be easier to relate our aims to Pendleton,[26] who has listed seven tasks to be achieved in the consultation. These are:

1   to define the reasons for the patient's attendance, including:

    –   the nature and history of the problems

    –   their aetiology

    –   the patient's ideas, concerns and expectations

    –   the effects of the problems

2   to consider other problems:

    –   continuing problems

    –   at-risk factors

3   to choose with the patient an appropriate action for each problem

4   to achieve a shared understanding of the problems with the patient

5   to involve the patient in the management and encourage the patient to accept appropriate responsibility

6   to use time and resources appropriately

7   to establish or maintain a relationship with the patient that helps to achieve other tasks.

Chronic care

In establishing novel ways of service delivery, treatment of patients requiring chronic care, such as those with asthma, provides some real advantages.

1 the reason for the consultation can be assumed, in as far as it relates to the asthma

2 outcome objectives may have already been agreed with the patient in previous consultations.

Adapting these ideas to SCAMP, our tasks for implementation of the system (in terms of the telemedicine consultation) become:

1 to define the patient's ideas, concerns and expectations together with the effects of the asthma on the patient

2 to achieve a shared understanding of asthma with the patient

3 to choose with the patient an appropriate action

4 to involve the patient in the management of the condition and encourage the patient to accept the appropriate responsibility

5 to use time and resources appropriately

6 to establish or maintain a relationship with the patient that helps to achieve the other tasks.

In terms of the Shale–Edwards model:

* 1 and 2 should be achieved in the consultation

* 3 and 4 should be achieved by determination of the health status of the patient, and the subsequent agreed plan

* 5 and 6 will be tests of the piloting and implementation of the project.

Patients and their advocates

If the patient's state of health is deemed to be unsatisfactory, what is the role of the advocate and who should that be? Synonyms of advocate are champion and supporter. All health care professionals should fulfil this role, but we see the possibility of a hierarchy operating, with those health care professionals who are geographically closer to the patient acting as advocates for the patient to those who are physically more remote.

SCAMP and telemedicine in action

In our view the majority of care will be provided in primary care, with a minimum data set and health status being collected for each patient on a regular basis. If the patient records 'unsatisfactory' on three consecutive consultations then a three-way teleconsultation will be arranged (sooner if required):

- the consultant will have access to all the data that have been collected

- the general practitioner's role as advocate will be to explain why the patient's health status is considered 'unsatisfactory'

- the outcome will be a management plan that has been agreed between all three parties

- if the patient has to attend the hospital then all three parties will know why the patient is attending

- the differing perspective that the health professionals bring to bear on the situation will provide education to all parties involved.

In this way we feel that the aims of combining SCAMP and telemedicine will have been met.

The future role of telemedicine

With the move towards the NHS becoming a primary care-led service and secondary care becoming a smaller highly specialized service (probably with fewer staff than currently), there is a need to ensure high standards of care across these sectors based on agreed standards and quality. To ensure this, health professionals based in the primary and secondary care sectors will need to work together more closely and to devise novel and innovative processes that allow more integrated activity.

The implementation of this model for the shared care of asthma is now well advanced, with software written that allows for a series of inputs by health professionals of varying grades. More importantly, there is a facility to allow input of data by the patient. The system uses the standards set out by the British Thoracic Society and the experience of both primary and secondary care workers in the field of asthma. The relationships between inputs by different health care professionals and the patient allow for a very flexible process that can be run either on paper or electronically. The latter system would allow doctors, nurses and patients sharing a distributed medical record to be separated by considerable distances. This has great implications for the future. Siting of care as close as possible to the patient and the primary care staff is seen to be in line with the shift of resources to primary care.

A combination of this process and the added benefit of a 'telemedicine' approach would result in a very powerful device that could be developed as an innovative hospital specialist outreach service. These could be sited in community hospitals or general practice (the location is now less relevant) to allow patients from the feeding network of general practitioners to be seen closer to home.

One-off or chronic care could be provided in this way. In the diagnosis of a patient with angina, a clinic with staff who are qualified to exclude aortic stenosis and can supervise exercise testing could be set up within the community. The consultant who 'reads' the test and conveys the results to the patient could be at a location which is many miles away.

Another example of this would be to offer an asthma/respiratory clinic based at a community hospital for local general practices. This could be run by a respiratory nurse specialist from the NHS Trust hospital, who would be linked to the distributed medical record network, as would the general practitioners and the consultant based at the NHS Trust hospital. Using a shared care protocol, the nurse could manage the majority of these patients and with telemedicine in place would have access to the consultant at the NHS Trust to allow problems to be discussed between consultant and nurse or patient, thereby reducing the need to refer the patient to the NHS Trust for consultation.

The implementation of SCAMP underpinned by:

- a distributed medical record network and

- telemedicine

has the following benefits:

1   patients have direct input to their care and an extra stake in health care

2   nurse practitioners become fully effective and take on the burden of the majority of the routine care of patients with asthma, yet maintaining the standard of care at a very high level

3   there is instant access to consultants both visually and electronically with regard to discussion and review of data

4   there will be important benefits for more precise training of staff both in the hospital and in general practice as there is the prospect of an immediate and prospective interface audit of care across the primary and secondary sectors

5   such audit can be very precise in terms of clinical standards, the effectiveness and efficiency of individual staff and cost-effectiveness

6   the ability to implement agreed protocols of care and to audit the process of care and the efficiency of the individual should reduce medical practice variation and maintain the quality of care delivered.

The business case for SCAMP

As in any resource-limited organization, the implementation of the SCAMP scheme was only possible after a business case had been prepared. This can be summarized as follows.

Mission statement
SCAMP is dedicated to ensuring that all health outcomes, as determined by every patient after consultation with their physician or nurse in regard of their asthma, are met.

Aim
Our aim is to introduce a system that will allow us to provide clinically efficient services as near as possible to the patient's home. Our emphasis must, therefore, be on the management of patients (taking full account of their views) that makes most appropriate use of professional skills rather than on location of care.

Goals
1   to ensure that all participating clinicians record a minimum data set of predetermined information at each consultation. This data set will be used during the consultation with all patients to decide their asthma status

2   to use existing, sophisticated technology to ensure that patients' health care records are available to clinicians at different locations on a real-time basis. Telemedicine will be integrated to facilitate communication between health professionals and patients in regard of patients' health needs

3   to endeavour to ensure that organizational and professional barriers are transcended, to ensure that the health outcomes that patient and clinician have jointly determined can be achieved in a clinically efficient manner

4   to provide a vehicle to ensure that the education, of both patient and clinician, will be meaningful and, by being delivered close to the point of care, integrated into the service provision of that care.

To deliver our aim, the following objectives need to be met:

• develop and implement agreed clinical guidelines for inclusion in contracts and use by clinical staff in delivering care

- determine the percentage of patients who are 'satisfactorily controlled' and 'unsatisfactorily controlled' at each contact, in both primary and secondary care, with a view to improving our baseline figures

- adopt a pragmatic approach that allows continual service development. We intend to change the focus of care from severity of illness to stability of illness, ensuring that the correct subpopulation of patients are in contact with the consultant at the appropriate time

- develop further versions of SCAMP software.

As part of the business planning exercise, the creators of SCAMP undertook a SWOT (strengths, weaknesses, opportunities, threats) analysis, the findings of which follow.

Strengths

- SCAMP is intellectually coherent

- SCAMP is patient-centred

- SCAMP is being implemented in a services environment

- SCAMP delivers measurable health outcomes

- ability to link and use telemedicine

- location of care becomes far less important than at present

- novel technology allows rapid, iterative prototyping

- software can be easily customized.

Weaknesses

- narrow base; few clinicians involved at present

- limited resources of both time and finance.

Opportunities

- a cascade strategy to roll out the system to:

    - more practices

    - more Trusts

    - other clinical areas

    - other health professional groups including educational needs

- involving other organizations

    - Medical Research Council

- charities

- pharmaceutical industry.

Threats
• other systems being developed to manage shared care.

SCAMP cascade strategy

As SCAMP is operated over a period to assess its effectiveness we intend, given the generic basis of the Shale–Edwards model, to examine options for introducing the concept into other clinical areas.

We know that the technology and infrastructure that underpins SCAMP works, and indeed we have successfully demonstrated the software to many interested parties, including the NHS Information Management Group (IMG) and visitors from overseas. However, we recognize that the cultural changes required to allow SCAMP to be widely implemented as a service tool are many and subtle, but we are confident of our cascade strategy to achieve them.

An alternative 'health career' for the patient

Mr Beaumont was a 56-year-old man with severe COPD when Dr Melbourne (primary care) and Dr Hardy (Consultant Respiratory Physician) agreed a shared care protocol encompassing agreed standards of care and criteria for transfer of care between the primary and secondary sector.

Background

When Dr Hardy first reviewed Mr Beaumont's clinical data they recorded a healthy childhood and adolescence with no evidence of respiratory disease. He had commenced smoking at the age of 15 years (1952) and apart from an episode of pneumonia in 1965 had no symptoms until he presented with cough and chronic sputum production to Dr Melbourne in 1973. There was an episode of pneumonia in 1975 and winter bronchitis in 1977; when it was recorded that he was still smoking 30 to 40 cigarettes per day. Other salient features recorded were three courses of antibiotics during the winter of 1979–80 when a firm diagnosis of chronic bronchitis was made. Dr Melbourne prescribed salbutamol and recorded there was little reversibility. The next winter led to exacerbations needing three courses of antibiotics plus one of oral prednisolone. Inhaled beclomethasone dipropionate was commenced in the following year. In 1983, two courses of antibiotics plus prednisolone were required and Mr Beaumont lost six weeks of work.

Following this it was recorded that his exercise tolerance had dropped to less than a hundred yards without stopping because of shortness of breath. He retired from work on health grounds at the age of 46 in 1983.

Secondary care

Dr Hardy confirmed Dr Melbourne's findings of irreversibility to β_2-agonists. In addition a formal steroid trial (prednisolone 30 mg OD for 14 days) showed no reversibility of FEV_1, or FVC. Nebulized therapy plus ipratropium bromide were introduced in 1985 and in 1989 it was clear that Mr Beaumont could not stop smoking without help.

Between 1989 and 1993 there was significant progression in Mr Beaumont's condition with first recorded loss of weight and an episode of congestive cardiac failure with type II respiratory failure in 1992. During 1992 and 1993 there were periods of clinical stability with diuretics and digoxin therapy with significant episodes of hypoxaemia being recorded on several occasions (lowest PaO_2 6.8 kPa). An assessment for long-term oxygen therapy showed a rise in the PaO_2 to 7.5 kPa on an F_IO_2 of 0.24 and a $PaCO_2$ of 6.5 kPa. At this time the FEV_1 was 0.86 litres with an FVC 1.35, though it was noted that the patient was barely able to blow for more than two seconds.

Impact of shared care

The development of shared care led to a new plan agreed between Mr Beaumont, Dr Melbourne and Dr Hardy with the primary intention of keeping Mr Beaumont at home and transferring as much of his care as possible to the primary sector, with Dr Hardy acting as a resource of specialist advice and activity should it be needed. The plan can be summarized as follows:

- oxygen therapy in excess of 16 hours per day at an F_IO_2 of 0.24

- nebulized salbutamol plus ipratropium bromide on a b.i.d. to q.i.d. regimen with a regular assessment of Mr Beaumont's condition and his ability to use the nebulizer appropriately by the practice nurse

- nutritional advice and the use of supplements assessed by the practice nurse based on advice obtained from the dietitian in the hospital sector

- smoking cessation counselling by the counsellor in the secondary care sector at a single visit then supported by telephone calls, leaflets and reinforcement by primary care staff visiting Mr Beaumont

- a reduction in outpatient visits to take into account the disability and level of disruption involved in getting Mr Beaumont to and from hospital

- provision of aids within the house including a stair lift and shower to improve the ability of Mr Beaumont to cope in his own home

- stand-by antibiotics for Mr Beaumont to start himself on the basis of advice provided by both primary and secondary care. This is to be assessed regularly by the practice nurse

- provision of a wheelchair to increase the mobility of Mr Beaumont both in and out of the house

- immunization on an annual basis for influenza and pneumococcal pneumonia.

Practicalities and outcomes

On the basis of these changes agreed between Dr Hardy, Dr Melbourne and Mr Beaumont it was possible to reduce hospital visits and to manage Mr Beaumont mainly within the community. The aim was to limit visits to an annual assessment at the hospital, unless it was necessary to respond to deterioration in his overall condition. An agreed annual assessment relating to blood gas analysis, assessment of nutritional state and review by the smoking cessation counsellor was all that was needed. Targets were also set to reduce the amount of antibiotic treatment if possible and to increase mobility and activity on the basis of the provision of a plan of shared care between primary and secondary sectors.

This approach makes the needs of the patient and his family paramount, with regard to normality of daily living and provides care as close as possible to the patient and, wherever possible, within his own home, while maintaining a high standard of care which previously would have been delivered primarily from the hospital sector. This agreement between all parties reduced the stress of the patient having to visit the hospital on numerous occasions, when very little might happen in terms of alteration in management. The shared care offered in this circumstance works primarily to the advantage of the patient and the maintenance of his health to the agreed best possible level in the community.

References

1 GRASSIC (1994) Integrated care for asthma; a clinical, social and economic evaluation. Br Med J 308, 559–564.

2 Ovretveit J (1992) Health Services Quality. Blackwell Special Products, Oxford.

3 Coulter A (1992) The patient's perspective. In Hospital Referrals (eds M Roland, A Coulter), p. 127. Oxford University Press, Oxford.

4 Grace J F, Armstrong D (1986) Referral to hospital: extent of agreement between the perceptions of patients, general practitioners and consultants. *Family Practice* **3**, 143–147.

5 Dowie R (1983) *General Practitioners and Consultants: a Study of Outpatient Referrals.* King Edward's Hospital Fund for London, London.

6 Jones R H (1989) Data collection in decision making: a study in general practice. *Med Ed* **21**, 99–104.

7 Wilkin D, Dornan C (1990) *General Practitioner Referrals to Hospital: a Review of Research and its Implications for Policy and Practice.* Centre for Primary Care Research, University of Manchester, Manchester.

8 Eddy D M (1990) Practice policies: where do they come from? *JAMA* **263**, 1265–1275.

9 Eddy D M (1990) Designing a practice policy: standards, guidelines and options. *JAMA* **263**, 3077–3084.

10 Sweeney B (1994) The referral system. *Br Med J* **309**, 1180–1181.

11 Bailey J, Black M, Wilkin W (1994) Specialist outreach clinics in general practice. *Br Med J* **308**, 1083.

12 Charlton B G (1993) Holistic medicine or the humane doctor. *Br J Gen Pract* **43**, 475–477.

13 Balint M (1957) *The Doctor, His Patient and The Illness*, pp. 69–80. Churchill Livingstone, Edinburgh.

14 Royal College of General Practitioners (1993) *Evidence to the Monopolies and Mergers Commission Inquiry into Private Medical Services.* Royal College of General Practitioners, London.

15 Welsh Health Planning Forum (1989) *Strategic Intent and Direction for the NHS in Wales.* WHPF, Cardiff.

16 Darley B, Griew A, McLoughlin K *et al.* (1994) *How to Keep a Clinical Confidence.* HMSO, London.

17 Korner E (1984) *The Protection and Maintenance of Confidentiality of Patient and Employee Data.* A Report from the Confidentiality Working Group. Steering Group on Health Services Information. HMSO, London.

18 Department of Health (1988) *Personal Social Services: Confidentiality of Personal Information.* Department of Health, London.

19 British Association of Social Workers (1986) *A Code of Ethics for Social Work*. British Association of Social Workers, London.

20 Donabedian A (1960) Evaluating the quality of medical care. *Millbank Memorial Fund Quarterly* **44**, 166–206.

21 Orali R, Harkey D, Edwards J (1995) *Byte* **20**(4), 108–122.

22 Pringle M (1989) What benefits do general practitioners see in electronic links to hospitals, family practitioner committees and community services? *Health Trends* **21**, 126–128.

23 NHS (1992) *The Clinical View of the Common Basic Specification. The Cosmos Project Clinical Process Model Version 2.0*. NHS Management Executive, Birmingham.

24 GRASSIC (1994) Effectiveness of routine self-monitoring of peak flow in patients with asthma. *Br Med J* **308**, 564–567.

25 Neighbour R (1987) *The Inner Consultation*. Kluwer Academic Publishers, London.

26 Pendleton D (1984) *The Consultation: an Approach to Learning and Teaching*. Oxford University Press, Oxford.

Index